Snow Lion's Delight

SNOW LION'S DELIGHT

108 Poems

SAKYONG MIPHAM

Introduction by Anne Waldman

Edited by Emily Hilburn Sell

The Kalapa Court

Halifax 2005

THE KALAPA COURT

an imprint of

VAJRADHATU PUBLICATIONS

1678 Barrington Street, Second Floor

Halifax, Nova Scotia

Canada B3J 2A2

(902) 421-1550

orders@shambhalashop.com

www.shambhalashop.com

PRINTED IN CANADA

Library and Archives Canada Cataloguing in Publication

Sakyong Mipham Rinpoche, 1962-
Snow lion's delight: 108 poems / Sakyong Mipham; introduction by
Anne Waldman; edited by Emily Hilburn Sell

Poems.
ISBN 1-55055-022-5

I. Sell, Emily Hilburn II. Title

PS3619.A428S6 2005   811'.6   C2005-906116-2

For Tseyang

Contents

Introduction by Anne Waldman ix

WHITE HORSE OF LHASANG 1

CAPE BRETON 2

TO MY FATHER'S CHILDREN 3

COME WITH ME 4

WHO IS KNOCKING? 5

OPENING 7

LOVE HAS CONQUERED THE SPARROW 8

SUMMER FLOWER 9

SUNSHINE IN THE PRAIRIES 10

TEARS FROM BEAUTY 11

DESTINY, GOOD MORNING 12

YOU YOU YOU IN PARIS 14

TIBETAN MEADOWS 16

LEAD ME BY THE HAND 18

WISDOM LIGHTNING BOLT 20

BLUE DRAGON 22

RUN WITH MIND 23

TOUCH MY FACE 25

WOLF IN MY EYES 26

GENUINE 28

SAND 29

WHY HIDE? 30

TOUCHING YOU 31

TERROR 32

CUTTING THE LIFE BLOOD 34

NIGHT IN KALAPA 35

LIFE SPINS AROUND 37

OPEN MY EYES 39

COUNT ME IN 41

TIME FLOATS, MEASURED 42

TIMELINESS 43

SAMBA 44

WIND GAVE BIRTH TO LIGHT 45

EU TE AMO 46

LHASANG 47

NOW 48

TUNQUÉN 49

GARUDA IS BORN 50

VICTORY CRY 51

KARMIC WIND 52

DONNA MEANS LADY 53

A HORSE WHOSE NAME IS WATER 54

A LITTLE HERE 55

TLGD 56

LIGHTNING STRUCK TWICE 57

DARLING 58

WALKING WITH THE ENLIGHTENED IN CELTIC 60

THE SUN, THE MOON, THE RIVER 62

BEHIND GOLD AND PURPLE 64

LIFE OFTEN GOES THAT WAY 66

OLD FRIEND 67

DUET 70

BLUE PLANET 73

MEADOWS IN HEAVEN 74

FORTUNATE BIRTH 76

DESPERATE 78

VAJRA FAREWELL 79

COME, COME, AND DANCE 80

RADIATING MIND 82

A SEED WAITING TO GROW 84

LADIES AND GENTLEMEN 85

PERFECT SWING 87

JUMP START 89

ISLAND PROCLAMATION 90

DRALAS ON YOUR SHOULDERS 91

MAGYAL POMRA 92

SWORD IN HAND 93

THOUGHTS 94

PEACE 96

THE SUN WILL SHINE 97

THE MOON 98

FEELING 99

ADVENTURE GREAT EASTERN SUN 101

TIMING 102

MIDSUMMER'S DAY 104

THINK TWICE AND BE HAPPY 105

THREE SORBETS 107

GOODBYE 108

HAPPINESS HA HA 110

GLIMPSE OF NATURE 112

QUANDARY 113

SECRET 114

STEAMBOAT SPRINGS 116

ON THE SPOT 117

HIGH-FIDELITY LOVE 118

MY FRIEND BARRY BOYCE 120

MARS IS HOT 121

HAPPY BIRTHDAY, MR. PRESIDENT! 122

BLUE, ALWAYS 123

THE HORIZON 124

BIRD'S EYE VIEW 125

CULMINATION 126

GOLDEN LOTUS 128

MAGIC SAID HELLO 130

KISS MY HEART 131

GROUND LUNGTA 133

HAGGIS AND BUBBLE AND SQUEAK 135

HELP OTHERS 137

STOP THE PAIN 138

WHAT ABOUT ME? 139

AH HUM 141

GIVE IT UP 143

POETRY FINDS A DANCING PARTNER 145

SHIWA ÖKAR AND THE VALLEY OF WHITE 146

RETURN 148

FREEDOM 150

THE OTHER SIDE OF A JASMINE CUP 152

HOOK OF DELIGHT 154

Glossary 157

About the Author 163

Introduction

"Pick up your pots and pans/Grab that meditation belt and walk this path," Sakyong Mipham Rinpoche cheerfully extols us in *Snow Lion's Delight*, a garland of 108 realization poems that examine the naïve mind as it self-consciously experiences itself growing to greater insight and delight. Initially the ubiquitous "I" is terrifyingly alone in its quest for knowledge and empowerment. In order to proceed, this "I" must travel through an investigative understanding of thorny ego and its projections. The "moment" trembles with potential. Dare we wake up and experience reality on the spot? Become gentle warriors beyond the incessant vacillation of hope, fear, and doubt? Find motivation in personal heartbreak that on a path of realization must inevitably extend to others? Realize the essential Buddhist axiom that all beings desire to be happy? That we are not alone in this pursuit?

At the center of this collection is the notion of *bodhichitta*—tender heart—as well as *maitri*—loving kindness towards oneself. And yet these simple tenets struggle for a place in the world, a world increasingly insensitive to a philosophical notion of compassion, hostile even to the word *compassion*, which has been euphemistically abused. We find ourselves both literally and psychologically in a warring, suffering world-zone inured to acts of kindness, yet desperately in need of them, whose denizens grow cynical by the day. A current "version" of reality based on aggression is upon us as we increasingly progress into a tragic Dark Age.

Sakyong Mipham, a major lineage holder in both the Buddhist and Shambhala traditions, insists in these heart songs again and again that this does not have to be the case, that we can radically shift our view, that we have choices, that we might open up and be inspired to help and serve the world, as he does, that we can be playful and imaginative and open:

Mars is hot
I feel freakish
The Buddha is red

Many of these pieces resonate sonorously with traditional Tibetan *dohas* (realization songs) as well, and the tropes and metaphors of a natural imagery of the wild—soaring garudas, stormy mountain peaks, meadows of wildflowers, replete with "clouds of concepts," tall trees, albeit the rugged haunted charnel ground of the psyche. But the lonely majestic "I" warms to the world in its next breath, and writes to celebrate and honor friends, family, and lovers with humor and intimate detail. The poems may be both terrifically "occasional" and ceremonial in the context of this contemporary, youthful meditation master who travels around the world giving of his heart and wisdom. Occasions might include commenting on a performance of *Antony and Cleopatra*, socializing in chic hotspots of Brazil or Paris, riding a horse with extraordinary mindfulness, or unabashedly enjoying a game of golf. One might wonder, Who is this guy? How does one resolve the seeming contradiction of spirituality and worldliness? How may a dharma teacher be such an energetic man of the world?

What is precious about this glimpse into the life of the mind of the Sakyong is the surprise and contradiction, as well as the tenacious conviction evidenced here that one can and should wake up on the spot and be totally present wherever one is. It is as if the "I" of these poems is Everyman, and this "I" might be any one of us—guileless, sentimental, even corny about love, yet basically "on the path."

Sakyong Mipham is thus able to transverse temporal and spiritual as well as East and West with a straightforward, confident, and generous ease. He carries the responsibility—the sacred duty and karma—of dharmic leadership into his writing path, exemplified here in your hand. He wants you to find him in the cosmic dance of the snow lion, frolicking in fields of virtue and genuine delight. You'd be remiss not to join in.

Anne Waldman
Shambhala Mountain Center
August 2005
Year of the Wood Bird

Snow Lion's Delight

THE WHITE HORSE OF LHASANG

The white horse of lhasang,
I kiss the delicate moon
On this evening of doubt and hesitation.
Rampant are the warriors in my heart,
Clothed in the armor of passion and possibility.

My heart bursts forth in full bloom—
Lotuses, dandelions, sunflowers,
Blue, purple, red, and white.
I am the messenger of those in need,
The Mukpo of love and luminosity.

Breathe, inhale.
When I see you, I see the early morning sun rise.
You have touched me—the earth, the soil, the rock.
You are elemental.
Mother Theresa sits quietly waiting for cessation.
Don't forget we need reliability and trust.

Life is full of delicate skin.
I lick and kiss its face.
I slide my fingers along its muscular rivers.
How can I say more?

I am open, betrayed, and loved.
Pity is my evening nightingale.
Jealousy haunts my knees
As the occasional mosquito bites my ankle!
Love, desire—that is a falling sun.
Don't forget this is the open plain of northern Colorado.

6 September 1997
Dalvay-by-the-Sea, Prince Edward Island

1

CAPE BRETON

The eagle garuda gulls of Cape Breton,
Osprey with their claws—
I love this place,
The mountain fortitude of holy ones who dance,
Expressing their fortune and predicament.

Love is the theme:
Morning sparrows, sandpipers, lazy kasung,
Bewildered administrators—
They try and try again.

The wild horses of Tibet graze,
Sucking the sweet grain.
Yaks roam, knowing they have three precious months
To hear the Gaelic tune.
Cape Breton, I love you.
Open my heart with your salty breeze.

September 1997
Cape Breton, Nova Scotia

TO MY FATHER'S CHILDREN

You are children of the same father,
Branches bound to a single root.
Time now for development, nurturing the soul.
Working the mid-shift, come into your own;
Help each other be different
As karma bursts
And ancient debris falls away.

Though the blister is open and painful,
You must continue to walk.
You—the child, the older child—
Are here to play with others.
Write your name in the sand.
Let the ocean wash it away.
Possessiveness is the virtue of mothers;
When children play, all they have is freedom.

Be aware.
Blades of grass allow the dew to slide.
Trees swallow the open wind.
Let blue sky be the only boundary.

21 September 1997
Boulder, Colorado

COME WITH ME

You have no idea—
Who are you to hold me?
I've always thought of you
As the most beautiful of night.

I hold a candle before me.
Love is ever-present.
I just love.
Why don't you discover this?

Dance with no idea, no hope.
I dance,
Falling like a nightingale before you,
Embarrassing myself like a shooting star.

Like the love of night,
Like time that never changed,
I'm here—don't you know me?

WHO IS KNOCKING?

Golden clouds billow,
Skylark circles sun.
I feel happy sitting up in bed.
The thought of tea inspires a dewdrop on the window.
Each day clouds form
And somebody knocks on my door.

Who is trying to get in?
The bird circles high in the sky;
Bright concentric rings of light descend.
Who is knocking on my mind?

The door is closed,
Keeping what should be inside in,
Keeping out the wild unknown.
Am I peeking at myself?
Or is someone knocking on my door?

The river flows unnoticed.
Thoughts billow:
White majestic cushions for the gods,
Dolphins in the sea.
The skylark turns and swirls, plays on clouds.
Someone's definitely knocking on the door.

Who would visit me now, and why?
As I inhale the fresh crisp early morning air,
The golden radiance of benevolent sun,
Thoughts, schemes, and fears
Keep knocking on my door.

One thought then another—
I'm busy, can't you see?
Why do you knock when I am in the sky,
Circling sun,
Gazing at turquoise water,
Playing in the light?

OPENING

I feel the opening of my heart—
Sky
Clouds
Moon—
Even the sun wants me to open.

Cool breeze on my face,
Hair wavering in wind,
All I can do is open.
My hands, my feet,
Deep in my stomach
I feel open.

All the world's moons,
The suns of my dreams,
Say, "Open."
Celestial message,
Heart learns to love its treasure
Only by tasting your sweetness.

LOVE HAS CONQUERED THE SPARROW

Love has conquered the sparrow.
Bravery has a tone of awkwardness.
The sky is clear today.
I do not wish to die.

18 February 1999
Cape Cod, Massachusetts

SUMMER FLOWER

A drink from mountain stream—
Lost water comes to haunt me.
Surrounding loneliness,
Mind peers into vast blue sky.
A distant yogin's love song plays upon my
    ears.
The silence of this valley
Sings the cry of liberation.

Mind paces like a caged tiger.
Heart drowns in inexpressible chasm.
Let us bring it all to the path of bodhi.
Let us climb this mountain of uncertainty.
Look!
Look again!
The sun is rising.
Its golden-orange hue commands us to exhale.

26 July 1999
Shambhala Mountain Center

SUNSHINE IN THE PRAIRIES

To hold you,
See your smile—
Bright, beautiful, brilliant.
I love your being:
Joy, delight, and holiday.
When I relax
You melt into my heart like snow
So thick it traps all movement.
Your love—
As it dissolves in me
I find the sun.

1999

TEARS FROM BEAUTY

When the mind plays tricks,
Who has the last laugh?
Who is tricking?
Who is tricked?

As the dance twirls
Like a leaf falling from an aspen,
No one knows where trickery
Will end—
Upon the earth?
Upon a consciousness that knows
That sunlight's glimmer,
Rare and quivering beauty,
Is light reflected on our tears?

When a red-winged blackbird
Takes flight through tears,
Each feather distinct,
Space performs its duty:
Watered beauty leaves vision
Like the grey anthers of a sunflower.

Eyes open,
I await contact.
Then I will make up my mind.

DESTINY, GOOD MORNING

The sun danced as I slid my hand
Across this blessed face,
Immortal remnant of childhood,
Mirror of mother and father.

As water glides
I shake my head and wonder,
What has happened?
Who have I become?
Why do I cleanse an illusion?

Childhood
Mistakes
Life before now—
All reflected in clear water
Caressing sun-soaked skin.
Will it also soothe my heart,
Mind's rainbow prism?
But memories persist.

Who am I?
What is this elixir
Moisture
Rock
Cactus
Leaf of life
Dance
Dream?
Why am I deprived?
Why am I a lucky star,
Silver in the sky?

Behind my eyelids
Questions rise and fall
Like the water I cup in my hands.
A thousand times—wash this face,
Look through these eyes
And say with this heart,
Good morning.
Good morning, mirage called "me."
Good morning, life.
Good morning, destiny.

20 February 2000
Halifax, Nova Scotia

YOU YOU YOU IN PARIS

Relentless sunshine—
Who are you to look at me?
Did I do something wrong?
Wow! You're crazy!

Daffodil, dandelion
Spring, summer—
What expectation!
Imprison journalism.

Flight of garuda
Haphazard birth
Paris at midnight.
Let's talk about the dance of mind,
Tumble and fall,
Just dance love's extremity.
What is this awakening?

Count my worry beads
OM VAJRASATTVA HUM
OM VAJRA GURU PADMA SIDDHI HUM
KI KI!
Where is my focus?
SO SO!
I'm wondering what everybody thinks.
ASHE LHA GYALO!
Who cares?

Jeremy gave transmission.
He is hopelessly in love.

I could trust him at one point—
Now he's just one oar of Cleopatra's reproductive boat.
He thinks his stomach will save him.
I can tell you now, his hair won't.

Springtime of love.
Here in Paris I am older and wiser,
Yet still enchanted by this city's coils of joy.
Why don't you just kiss me
And say, "Je t'adore"?
Why not just jump out
And say, "I've been waiting for you"?

Wonderment
Time
Closeness
Paris
Shambhala—
I love you you you.
Beyond everything,
You hold me back and draw me in.

16 May 2000
Paris

TIBETAN MEADOWS

High in the meadows of Tibet
A white horse dances in the clouds,
Playing with the wind.
This land is rich:
Juniper, snow mountains, wildflower meadows.
It is birth ground, the earth and sky of goodness.

At dawn, five great suns shown—
Wisdom of all beings.
The moon sits high in vast blue sky—
Compassion of all beings.
The union of sun and moon arises
When humans trust their nature.

Wisdom and compassion are innately ours,
But these times challenge us.
Caught in agitated mind
Quick to use anger as solution
Consumed by what we want, never satisfied—
Our life force wanes and love abandons us.

For Shambhala warriors
Tenderness is the best weapon:
It annihilates materialistic fog,
Blows open the prison of selfishness,
Revolutionizes destiny.
The Prince of Warriors,
Awakened One who dared to conquer petty mind,
Proclaimed this truth, our legacy.

Let us be Shambhala warriors who see the good of all.
We have the power to let the selfless turquoise dragon play,
To frolic in snow lion's delight,
To follow tiger's meek, courageous steps,
To overcome our fear by letting go
Like the garuda who soars in cosmic space.
Let this be humanity's true calling—
To gather strength as warriors.

18 June 2000
Boulder, Colorado

LEAD ME BY THE HAND

What has become of me?
 The tide of equality has changed.
The scattering of summer's terns and 'pipers,
The waves the moon drew,
Are timed to my heartbeat.

Why does this balance, nature's interplay,
Change so dramatically
When I slide my eyes along a blade of grass?
Stem, stalk, and leaf
Welcome and embrace me.
Responsibility, cosmic delight, and spiritual weight
Beckon.

If this balance shifts,
Water will not meet my face;
The movement of air,
The beauty of spring sun and summer vapors,
Will not take body and soul to mountain heavens
Where the dance of time
Does not rob youth of life itself.

I am beyond this triangulation—
Don't try to capture me with haphazard sentiment.
Don't lie to someone who has seen the truth.
I revel in nondeception.
Count me in when buffalo gather,
When the wild horse has been tamed.
A warrior whose face was painted long ago,
Dancing, I move like a river in the sky.

Homecoming has been sweet.
It touches my lips and heaven no longer hides.
This journey began with its own elixir,
A golden hue I did not see before.
Now it returns me to the source.

WISDOM LIGHTNING BOLT

A bolt of wisdom struck my conceptual mind.
A sudden flash of insight—
Pause, moment
Beautiful, pristine
Unfabricated, natural—
Leaves me alone.
Without thought I remain motionless,
Infused by playful energy.

In this moment of silence
Who am I?
This flash has shown my mind,
Shattered the clouds of concept.

Who experienced what?
For a moment I was groundless, homeless—
A wanderer, a bird with no nest.
Uncomfortable in that freedom,
I tried to orient myself.

Why can't I relax with who I am?
Am I scared of being free?
So self-conscious that I cannot let the boundaries dissolve?
So small that I cannot jump?

I feel brave, but when wisdom presents itself
I hold back like an animal caught in bright lights.
This bright light is wisdom from within.
My whole life, longing to deepen—
When the moment comes, can I be ready?

I must prepare the ground.
A flash of wisdom comes not once or twice—
It is always available.
Can I open my eyes,
Slow down ever so slightly
And let its rush of energy, joy, strength
Ignite my heart and mind?

This flash is true being,
The nature of mind and heart.
Depression, anger, jealousy
Are speed's reflections,
Buzzing mind unable to relax.
These emotions invade and torment me,
Ransack my inner dignity.

Confusion's veil is just a garment to discard.
Strength to do so comes from meditation,
Engaging in the Buddha's path.
Warriors' courage works with mind,
Thinks of others,
Lets actions lay bare
The power and profundity of being.

To be ourselves—
Cut through the veil of aggression,
Smell the highland flowers,
Experience compassion, love, wisdom,
Meadows, trees, and sky—
This is the path that awaits us.

26 June 2000
Shambhala Mountain Center

BLUE DRAGON

Blue Dragon soars above the jewel of dharma,
Awakening love and compassion
With profound and noteworthy implications.
We must take this home, this nest,
And show it to the world
So all may know its secret beauty.
In thirty years the energy has risen
From Tiger's tail to Dragon's head—
Now all the dignities rejoice.

In response, we reflect the Great Eastern Sun
That has always shone in our being.
This realization is worth celebrating.
Cheerful thirtieth anniversary,
Tail of the Tiger/Karmê-Chöling!

23 July 2000
Karmê-Chöling

RUNNING WITH MIND

Mindfulness chases me like a wolf.
Time
Spring
Love
Doubt:
In this moment I can feel you holding me.
Let me guess,
Let me hope—
You arose from love.

What I dream to be is bear—
Proud, a lover of sweets contaminated by its beautiful fur—
Magnificent, black, and simply irresistible.
Nature has its tarts.
I fell for this seduction,
Wishing to lick it with my heart.

Can I rise naïve
Like a mountain snowstorm?
The puma within me—
Proud but simple lion who flees across majestic pleasure's
    meadowed mountain—
Waits to proclaim mastery of its territory,
Shambhala Mountain Center.

Join us, beautiful lion.
Join us, courageous bear.
Join Mipham, unconquerable in the vow to conquer suffering.
Join Sakyong, protector of Earth.

Let me help you, lion and bear—
If I cannot, who shall?

30 July 2000
Cheyenne, Wyoming

TOUCH MY FACE

Blue sky, dark and mesmerizing,
All encompassing, tantalizing, without beginning or end,
Blue, deep blue, a brilliant dark blue—
It captivates my mind.

Even the ground says, "Look at this enchanting sky."
The bones of my body,
Muscles that welcome oxygen and blood—
Energy overwhelms the heart who inhabits their
    miracles.

Gazing into fathomless blue sky, morning sky,
I melt away.
There is no person—
Only lover
Simple being
Heart and mind
Remain.

Within intimacy
Vibrant universal energy gives me strength.
Mind melts into self-possession
That wants to reach the depths,
Reality's frontiers.

Sipping life's juice
I know why sky is blue and deep, encompassing all.
The magician who cast a spell
Is sky itself.

WOLF IN MY EYES

The power of being alone can be measured
By how well I sit by myself.
Can I sit in a circle and watch my mind
Surrounded by a ring of mirrors that reflect
Me upon me
Self upon self
Thought upon thought
Hope upon hope
Self-reflection upon self-reflection?

When I sit in this space
Am I sitting alone with myself?
How alone is this sense of desolation?
Why is it that I feel surrounded
When I am alone?
I do not see these mirrors that reflect
The perplexed face of a lonesome self.

When I look at myself
I see a mountain rich in snow and timber
Gleaming in sunlight,
Wearing clouds like a cape,
Gazing in a clear blue mountain lake.
This mountain—pristine, desolate—
Is happy to watch its own reflection.
Mesmerized by solitude day and night
Among stars' galaxy of light,
It knows its place as a single mountain.
It knows itself by what it sees.

Crystal is what I see when I sit on my own.
I am by myself

Surrounded by a world of mirrors.
Among reflections
Who is alone?
Within perpetual insistence on
     independence
Which reflection is independent?
Which lake can separate itself
From the mountain it reflects?

In this play of perception lies reality.
What is the lake?
Who is the mountain?
Who am I to sit here by myself
Thinking I'm alone?
Without the lake's pristine reflection
I would not know I'm alone
Nor what loneliness is.
As summer winds blow
Grass bends, the golden wheat-field
     shimmers.
The sun reflects and sees its brightness.

The world
Life
Is born from its own reflection.
Move
Eat
Laugh
Hug—
Express a simple being
Dancing with its own reflections.
Being alone is the beginning
Of loving another.

GENUINE

I love my staff and they love me.

Genuineness—
Each day they work hard for me.
Each day they work hard for you.

Beauty—
They are so beautiful.
Their beauty shows compassion.

Strength—
They are the strongest.
I am proud of their strength.

Grace—
Under pressure they can say yes and even no.

This summer they have been beautiful, strong, and graceful
But most of all they have been genuine:
Genuinely terrified
Genuinely loving
Genuinely bewildered
Genuinely confused
Genuinely understanding.
In the end they are completely genuine.

I as a Mukpo have known many.
I as a Mukpo have known some very well.
But as a Mukpo I love the genuine.
I love my staff because they are genuine.

22 August 2000
Shambhala Mountain Center

SAND

In hot sun
I ride my horse.
It knows my heart.
Each hoof penetrates the sand.
Each shift in direction is a moment of insecurity—
Each breath, a love I never knew.
The saddle glides on this powerful horse.
The leather on its back hurts me.
The beast, the man—exhilarated.

I am nature
Force
Life.
That is why I ride the wind,
This energy called horse.

Riding
Taming
Conquering—
All in vain.
Never will I master the horse!
Only for an instant will hoof-print energy
Synchronize its heartbeat with mine.

Moment in time and space
Unrestrained by concept,
This magic is a dream
Never to awaken.

9 September 2000
Whistler, British Columbia

WHY HIDE?

Why be mysterious?
Beneath, buried deep,
Is it love?
Do you care?

Why do we hide?
My shoulder, stomach, chest
I tried to hide.
I even tried to hide the sky and noontime sun.
Who am I shunning?
Who is proclaiming a flash of insecurity?

Am I scared?
Frustrated?
Do harsh words conceal inhibitions,
Inner hopes and fears?

Could I be a wildflower unashamed—
Let anyone touch me
Smell me
Hold me?

Can I be wild beyond thought and concept?
Can I be a beautiful flower and expect nothing?

I am part of nature.
Without losing my inner beauty
Can I be open?

9 September 2000
Whistler, British Columbia

TOUCHING YOU

Little things I tell you,
The scratch on my back—
I look
And you know.

Shadow
Telephone
Morning bird—
You know.

Rain falls on my window.
On my heart,
Sunshine glimmers.
I feel you in sky,
In wind rustling clothes.
I think you know how I feel.
The distant look—I see you.
I put my hand upon each tear
And realize you are there.

9 September 2000
Whistler, British Columbia

TERROR

Terror is a love of its own.
All the terror in the world will never satisfy us.
Beyond comprehension
Terror leaves us in shock.

Don't you ever wonder why
People are scared of unpredicted events,
    unfulfilled expectations?
Terror is a fact of life.

What if we could conquer terror?
What if terror had no power?
What if terror was simply a puddle on a path
A dewdrop of conceptuality
A mystery that was solved
A piece of bread?
What if terror itself was no more than steam
    rising from a cup of tea?

If terror was a piece of corn we bit into
A stone we skipped
A field we walked through
A mountain we could climb
A pet we could love—
If terror was simply a part of our mind
A part of our heart for which we had no use
A part of our psyche—only a myth we believe
    in—
Would all life be captivated by fear?

Leave it.

Let it go.

Love as though it never began.

Terror, love—

This simple association was never born.

Why hold it to be truth?

Why proclaim it to be ultimate?

What if terror was nothing but an umbrella we
   never opened

A siren we never heard

A butterfly we never caught

A lover we never touched

A moon we never saw?

What if the only planet we knew was called
   Confidence?

9 September 2000
Whistler, British Columbia

CUTTING THE LIFE BLOOD

Coming and going,
Summer and winter:
What can I learn from dualism?
What can I learn from my own language—
A language that says
To go from here to there?
Does this melody reverberate in every traveler?
Where is it that I go?
Where did I come from?

Trapped,
I know I must go,
Leaving something behind.

Like a bluebird at dawn
The colors are vivid.
Yet when bird flies through sky
Blueness collides
And journey vanishes.

The journey that awaits
Takes place in antiquity,
Its origins, like this morning,
Impossible to trace.
When did darkness turn to light?

Let me hold my breath and say,
"This adventure may lead to a land
That has yet to be named,
But that might be at my fingertips."

February 2001
Cape Cod, Massachusetts

NIGHT IN KALAPA
(For Emily Sell)

This time it happened—
Caught in a thunderstorm,
I spun and twirled.
I was dizzy
I was happy
I was caught off guard.
This whirlwind took my heart.

I needed everything to fall apart
Like feathers from a pillow
Tossed high into the sky.
Everything comes falling down
Gliding on a breeze caught in its own time—
Energy that can't be measured.

Comet shoots across my existence.
This wonderful force does not know where it will go.
I need things to fall apart.
I want things to fall apart.
All through time, all through the day
I have held on and held on tight.
Now everything falls apart.

The sun and moon know how to fall apart.
Spring knows how to be summer.
Autumn leaves know how to fall.
Can I be like the seasons
And know that falling apart
Is the movement of time,
The movement of life?

I have not given up,
I have simply woken up.
This wild burst of energy
Wants to twirl and spin.
It wants mayhem.

I am mayhem—
Claustrophobia self-liberated,
Hesitation with a friend called fathomlessness.
I am that smile that shines across the sky.
If you look up you will see me
And fall apart.

3 March 2001
Halifax, Nova Scotia

LIFE SPINS AROUND

In tumultuous times the mind speaks incoherently.
Suddenly the topics are as varied and unpredictable
As a monkey jumping on a crocodile.
We might blurt out, "I love you!"
Yell, "I hate you!"
Rehearse a tone that says, "Thank goodness,"
Or sigh, "Oh no!"

In this foggy realm of haphazard thought
There is no clear direction—
Even a compass loses its ground.
We are in the vortex of lifestreams,
Energies with no beginning that determine what happens now.
When they collide,
We find ourselves confined by their company.

Then we wallow and indulge
In the confluence of too many rivers:
Thoughts of what we should and shouldn't have done
Courageous acts we could have undertaken
Flowers we forgot to look at
People we meant to kiss
Fish we wanted to release
Dreams we might have made real.

Thoughts create the fog that overwhelms us.
From this mist arise the buffalo we ride,
With wild wind gusting from their nostrils.
Like birds engulfing us with flapping wings,
Thoughts keep swirling
And we spin.

Unless we make a graceful exit
This swamp consumes us.

There is no solution,
No correct direction.
When the mist takes over
We must realize that these confluences
Are generated by mind.

Our hearts are like a turtle—
Hard on the outside, soft on the inside.
Occasionally we poke our heads out
And wonder how to move beyond our murky quagmire.

When such desire arises,
Be primordial.
Recognize truth,
Take a step forward.

Understand confusion.
Acknowledge the process
Like a tiger putting paws to earth.
Neither shunning nor indulging thoughts,
Keep moving.

Don't stop to weigh confusion's pros and cons.
Take human-sized steps,
Fortified by primordial confidence.
Then the sun will rise.

8 March 2001
Hubbards, Nova Scotia

OPEN MY EYES

From bliss the radiant sun of Chökyi Gyatso
Performs a vajra dance,
Gathering dakinis with its movement.
Karma's turbulent wind provides yak-dung fuel
For the warrior whose smile releases windhorse.

A drop of bliss rides the wind,
Eternally raining love into our hands.
As each of us awakens
We find the pure domain:
Vajra sky, song, and joy.

Dharmakaya—potent confluence.
Release from samsara—great gathering of virtue,
Offering-worthy mountain.
Bodhichitta propels us step by step
Through mammoth display—universal union.
Let the bhumis tie each hair on our head into a jewel-like knot.
Let our eyes radiate bodhichitta like the sun and the moon
As we join Samantabhadra.

The dreamlike boy who rose from the sacred dirt of eastern Tibet
Came to this powerful land,
Opened his heart, gushed forth jewels,
Footsteps resounding like dharma drum.
Precious manifestation, Dombi Heruka,
When you tossed your skull cup
Into the whirlwind of past and present,
Could you have predicted that amrita would land in our hearts?

Take the pregnant tigress.
Gather the reins of drala.
Be mother and father, brother and sister,
Heaven and earth.
Do not forget your humor!
Please guide these children to the Great Eastern Sun.
Remain in the Vajra Stupa, emanating and gathering,
An ever-present monument to courage.

28 July 2001
Shambhala Mountain Center

COUNT ME IN

Happiness slips between my fingers.
Don't you realize
I'm a dog who has seen the sun,
A lover who knows
Why time transcends the human realm?
I like to daydream about life
As sweet as pineapple.
I am your heaven.
Count me in,
Because all I love
Is seeing my horses run free.

18 August 2001
Shambhala Mountain Center

TIME FLOATS, MEASURED

When this yogin of mahamudra cast a sail
He could jump on the back of a seagull,
Catch jetstreams, tornadoes, currents,
Pressure, wind, and energy,
Flutter and fluster every feather.

The sun shone and I dove,
Sailing beyond thought,
Beyond hesitation,
Beyond expectation.

When I sailed from the land of concept
I did not know what I was doing or why.
In this seminal act
I felt the fever of failing,
Not knowing where the tides of wind would take me.

Humanity was created by warriors
Who did not doubt their own prowess.
Life is created by special delight—
Look at my face and kiss me.
I can help if you give me the chance.

27 October 2001
Vermont

TIMELINESS

The winter brothers
Calm and Happiness
Express themselves as Suchness,
Bound by golden cufflinks
Known as Virtue.

When I fall back into cool blue virgin lake
Everything I knew about space and time dissolves
As bubbles float towards heaven from my face.
The love trapped under knows no language.

Flakes of happiness fall off the donkey named Surprise.
Can you guarantee enlightenment if I drink this milk?

27 October 2001
Vermont

SAMBA

Summer became winter
Cold is home
Mind is heart
Dance is meditation
Brazil is mind
Heat is heart
Love is mind and heart
Compassion is Brazil
Time is doubt
Rhythm is hope
Time is life
Jump
Beauty
Emotion
Energy
Life
Brazil
Shambhala.

18 March 2002
São Paulo, Brazil

WIND GIVES BIRTH TO LIGHT

Wind swinging willows
Gives birth to light.
A friend in a yellow jacket whispers,
"Dance and swim."
Mirror catches hesitation.
I see and cringe with heavy exuberance.
Out of this confusion
Your face is born.

18 March 2002
São Paulo, Brazil

EU TE AMO

Thunder crossed majestic sky.
With no friend, no enemy,
It roared, "I'm loud."

Rain:
No doubt or hesitation—
Timing was never an issue.
The sky fell
And I felt every drop.

São Paolo was being awakened.
São Paolo was discovering a new dawn.
How can I ignore this beautiful city?

I'm here for you.
Are you ready for me?
Sometimes you doubt your own heart.

Let's swim in the rain and hold hands.
This dance is eternal, like my love for you.
I love you, São Paolo.
Do you love me?

18 March 2002
São Paulo, Brazil

LHASANG

The time in passage
Caught the sailing beauty;
A mind known as Camelot
Shone in every gaze.
I presented exertion and discipline.

Infantile action—
Round
Square
Triangular—
Tears crying
Pain.

Walk forward—
Follow the man in front.
I hope to invoke the dralas,
By chance trip upon dignity,
By luck discover richness,
By karma complete the circle.
The sun shines today,
Reflecting our direction:
Lhasang.

18 March 2002
São Paulo, Brazil

NOW

A wild yak catches its horn
A truck grinds its gears
A groom raises the veil of a beautiful bride
Somebody rushes to the grocery store
A child cries
A great actor is rewarded
A king falls in love
Geese flying south rest at the eighteenth hole
A gorgeous girl gets kissed
A politician discovers sarcasm
A teacher discovers meaninglessness
A general loses the battle
I make love
You make apple pie
Everyone will die.

18 March 2002
São Paulo, Brazil

TUNQUÉN

Leaving Santiago
I've left half the population of Chile.
Now I'll discover the rest.
I'll start in Tunquén
At Raul's brown cottage on the South Pacific Ocean.

What surprise!
The land is enchanting, distinct,
Gentle and harsh simultaneously.
Dry air is infused by the sea.
Horses galloping freely
Fill my heart with skipped beats.

I want to ride the horse
Smell the sea
Feel the sun
Touch the earth
Gaze at wildflowers
Inhale the gardens of Chileans who have sneaked away
    to be at peace and find themselves.

I have found myself.
What delight, for I am in Tunquén.
I may not have discovered the other half of Chile,
But two birds flying into pale blue sky
Show me a good beginning.

3 April 2002
Tunquén, Chile

GARUDA IS BORN

Wait for birth, want birth—
Anticipation and anxiety
Come from the unknown.
Can we let go?

Will it be painful?
Just waiting for birth tries our patience.
We might have worked hard to create birth,
Waiting for the climax of operatic theater.
Or birth might unexpectedly
Fall like flowers from sky.

But actual birth stops us in our tracks.
Our mind is liberated
Senseless
Without orientation
Stranded in all-pervasive joy, wonder,
    disbelief.

Enjoy birth, for it arises
From circumstances beyond our grasp.
Let go, spread your wings.
See that we are garuda—
Mystic creature fully born,
Here to consume the three worlds.

That is the reality.

3 April 2002
Tunquén, Chile

VICTORY CRY

The Southern Cone
Leaps from past to future.
Seeds cast upon the ground
Have fermented into amrita,
Intoxicating dharma
Nurtured by love and sweat
As precious hands formed anjali.
There's no doubt now—
The mix of Latin and Shakyamuni
Is here to stay.
The confluence of the Rigdens' blood
And hot empañadas
Broke us free from our cocoon.
Now our victory cry resounds
From the Southern Hemisphere.

3 April 2002
Tunquén, Chile

KARMIC WIND

Trade winds blew my karmic sail
Far from home
Far from anywhere.

Now I return
Expecting sweet smell of sun and love,
Unknown minds rich with potential
Surrounded by nerves.

I return with a secret mission:
A task, a love, a journey
Known as bodhichitta—
Life's milk, honey so sweet
It falls from the hearts of the dakinis
Landing in the mindstream of awareness.

Dancing dralas circle us
When we take bodhichitta as our life.
Wind creatures, white, play instruments.
Flags flutter.
Such karmic wind has carried me here.

I'm not so far from home.
In fact I never left.
If only you would join me
On this heart's journey.

3 April 2002
Tunquén, Chile

DONNA MEANS LADY
(For Donna Hanczaryk)

Summer has three suns.
One is Donna.
When I look at her I want to protect her,
My sister who cannot swim.

The moon is full.
Donna gives me advice.
She is Mother Moon,
The passage of time.

When I have a hard time breathing
Donna tells me to inhale.
When I lie under the stars
Donna comes over me like a blanket.
All is dark except for her.
This time I find myself—
Hot, tired, refreshed, hopeful.

This is the country of Donna.
Love comes at unexpected times;
Time moves at its will.
This love I feel for you
I feel for everyone.

Donna is the power in ourselves we can draw from
Like a well deep in the desert.
I call her name as it echoes in the space above me.
I am grateful for someone to call Donna.

5 May 2002
La Romana, Dominican Republic

A HORSE WHOSE NAME IS WATER

Across the Great Plains
 I ride the horse of excitement,
Nomad's daughter knows how to kiss me.
A wave of seduction stops me from biting my own lip.
The forward journey of indispensable desire
Begins with my hips.
This lover seeks true seduction unbound by gravity.
You are the fool who does not believe this.

Lamenting my past actions, everyone dives into chicken soup,
Broth made by constant reminders.
Don't hold me—
This beauty is me.
I ride a horse whose name is water.
The bit, the saddle, the mane is all you gave me.
Don't be surprised.
You're the one who asked me to dance.

6 May 2002
La Romana, Dominican Republic

A LITTLE HERE

A little here, a little there.
A skootch here, a shove there.
A bit to the left, a bit to the right.
Up a little, down a little.
A nudge to this side.
A dash up, a dash down—
Keep going.
A bit to the left, a bit to the right—
You're pretty close, you've almost got it.
Don't stop now.
Not quite there, up a little bit, keep going.
That's it!
Don't stop now.

8 May 2002
La Romana, Dominican Republic

TLGD

When I run
Garuda chases me.
This mythic bird,
Terrifying and invigorating,
Spreads its wings
And sunlight, not shadow,
Flies in all directions.

When I breathe
My pounding heart,
Snow Lion within,
Roars to the conviction
I'm alive.
It will not let me die.

My feet are Tiger,
Aware of the earth,
Willing to respond
When I feel danger:
Instinct is my blood.

My mind is Dragon,
Pervading all the skies.
Even heaven is consumed.
Fathomless perception guides me.

I am courage, never knowing fear.
Thunder and lightning
Are my smiles and laughter.
All this before breakfast!

22 May 2002
Dechen Chöling

LIGHTNING STRUCK TWICE

Lightning struck twice.
This little chateau could not see it coming.
Spring wanted to stick its head out and shout,
"I am here!"

But English duty fell upon the French house;
Though brilliant sunshine was everywhere,
Celtic rain fell,
A steady drizzle—
Bliss for meditators,
Boredom for the frivolous.

Happy to be in St. Victurnien,
Here at the crossroads
We celebrate separation and growth.
Here I am, the young Sakyong,
Ready to tell passersby
Love is worth a thought or two.
I am the old Mukpo
Whispering compassion as an ancient hymn:
Let's put our hands together,
Respectfully bow our heads
And proclaim our beating heart.

22 May 2002
Dechen Chöling

DARLING

I feel Darling at my gate—
She is who I look for.
In the distance I see her
Perfect, radiating beauty all around.

Eyes weep
Heart swells
Lungs fill
Muscles are invigorated.
This is Darling,
The perfection.

Where is diamond perception?
In each direction excellence pervades.
This vision haunts me every morning:
I wonder why it isn't mine.
Then I discover the drala of white light.
She is the sparkle in my eye,
The blood of my heart.

Dreams
Mirages
Hallucinations
Hot sweat burning, full of fever.
I cannot see clearly.
Reaching out
I want to grab the rainbow,
Jump into a fresh spring pond, clear blue.

I wake up.
I am sitting on my meditation cushion.
Now it is time to discover this purity without dreaming.
I am warrior
Spiritual practitioner
The young person
The old one.
Life and dream are not so different.
Darling, I love you.

22 May 2002
Dechen Chöling

WALKING WITH THE ENLIGHTENED IN CELTIC

Sitting in the valley of Arthur,
The winds of history fall upon my face,
This Celtic land covered in blood springs forth—
Green meadows, sheep flying from valley to valley.
In this song of bewilderment, acknowledgement falls like mist.
This land is haunted, yet I feel awake,
Like a picture, the ideal.
Everything is perfect to my gaze.
When I ran through this valley,
A new magic was no concoction of John Dee. *

Swallowing my tied-and-bound fate
And friends have brought me here.
It was not the simple retreat of Peter and Jim, but the Gaelic wizards.
They had concocted a stew—
A bit of Arthur, of Gesar, Christian wisdom, and Buddhist
  compassion.
That is why the grass is so green.

This Mukpo nomad has seen the meadows of the world
And now triumph's weekend for a queen who trusted luck, **
Whose heritage has survived fifty years.
May the glory of Britain wipe out the suffering of less noble lands!

I heard the sound of compassion in a boat heading towards the
  river Avon.
Come with me! Look with me! Hear with me!
We are fortunate fools who can laugh.
When we exhale our tethered secrets

We arrive at the present moment, at the Now, the Must—
That is the intoxication of two cultures.

This is where I stand:
Between the river of Then and the mindstream of Now.
You are the benefactor; I am the acknowledger.
Don't just consume but give.
I have given—that is what my blood tells me.
I believe that is what you want.
Climb this little hill with me.
As we look, mist shrouds the dilemma of past and future.
Let us sit and cry and smile.

The Sakyong sighted from Litton hill the birthplace of John Dee, magus and court astrologer to Elizabeth I.

** *Written on the Golden Jubilee of Elizabeth II.*

2 June 2002
Cascob, Wales

THE SUN, THE MOON, THE RIVER

A sharp moment is when someone has told you the truth.
A dull moment is when you try to respond.
Being a lover—or trying to love—is full of daydreaming.
When Cleopatra oozes her affection,
Cuts it with her tempered wisdom
And exclaims, "You are not worthy of love and infatuation!"
That is the time a thousand years of manhood,
A thousand years of history and foundation,
Come crumbling down.

Out of this rubble, arise with grace and integrity.
Don't be bashful about your most secret hidden inhibitions,
For she is woman and you are man.
Power is on your side—skill with her.
At this moment do not touch your wounded heart or corrupt
   pride:
Put forth a face of gaiety and mirth.
Look at her—look at yourself,
For she sees you—now see her.

The Nile is wide but parts are shallow:
Cross it when you can.
Don't be foolish and drink from the serpentine river,
For she will win, and you will lose.
Because change is her blood,
You must be like the desert and move as the winds say.
This is a perpetual dance of mind and heart, of hard and soft.
Don't stand still:
The quicksand of discursive intention
Will make you sink.

Time helps neither you nor her,
But flexibility can wound this eternal play.
Be the sun, brilliant and wise.
Let her be the moon, brilliant and clear.
Between the two, life can be interesting.

2 June 2002
After a performance of Antony & Cleopatra
Cascob, Wales

BEHIND GOLD AND PURPLE

The running of time in evolution with Paris
Is the confluence of many rivers,
Past and future desires set free.
They run the streets like bulls—
Sharp horns, massive energy, strong hearts,
Days knowing they are loved.

My time in this vast city is meaningful
Because everyone needs to know
How to handle the mind,
How to understand the heart.
This is the beauty of Mukpo tantra.

The continuous stream of clan finds every corner.
When we taste it, our eyes open.
We are no longer beasts, animals to our senses—
We become truly Parisian.
On our shoulders, garudas cry.
In our hearts, dragons beat ancient drums.

This drama, this evening among friends,
Is so beyond the individuals present.
We are all delighted and consumed.
The light that touched us is in our eyes—
This stroke of magic brought us to life
Because we love the underlying factor of life.
No one talks about it, but in silence
We look into each other's eyes and feel it.

Don't run.
Dance, cry for love, because all of this—
Frivolity, insecurity, inhibition—
Relies upon the basic nature.
Sing if you want to
But let the blood percolate to the surface.
That redness
That part of this evening
That discovery—
Monumental, subtle, powerful—
Is our realization:
We are under the influence of the Mukpo clan,
Royal gold and purple.

Behind gold and purple we are all intimate—
Time does not separate us.
So we gather tonight
Opened out beneath it all.
Dynamic energy—France and Shambhala—
It is so simple that it may seem complicated.
That is why we must just sit,
Look at the sun and moon,
And see we are sitting at home.
This round table is made of friendship.
Hold my hand—
We are doing something no one knows.

10 June 2002
Paris

LIFE OFTEN GOES THAT WAY

One day I catch my keys before they fall.
Another day I thank a stranger
Who catches them for me.
He looks up grateful and surprised—
Life often goes this way.

At times I become passionate,
Fixating on someone hoping she loves me.
She looks at me and asks my name.
I say, "My name is Life."
She says, "Life often goes that way."

When I comb my hair,
I think I missed something,
But the mirror says,
"Life often goes that way."

At times the sun shines.
At others lightning thunders.
Rain comes down.
Winter becomes spring and summer.
Life often goes that way.

When I touch the earth,
Sit upon the ground, this fertile soil,
I realize I am so alone—
No one knows how I feel.
Life goes that way for everyone.

10 June 2002
Paris

OLD FRIEND

Your age provokes my madness.
Consumed by appearance
I look at you and become frightened.
Ten years have passed
Since I've seen
Touched
Or felt you.
In memory you are pure youth,
Beautiful and nimble,
Fountain of practical jokes.
Eternity was your message.

Encountering you this rainy Sunday,
I am shocked by your grey.
Where did sunshine go?
You and sun, you and moon, were one,
Now you and sadness, you and death
    are one.
Am I morbid? Am I scared?

I call your name.
You smile and look at me.
Suddenly your youth comes forward—
The frown on your face
Age in your skin
Grey in your hair
Dissolve.
They are joy.
I feel reunited—
You, me, our past present future—

Nothing has changed.
I love you:
This moment, our friendship.
Age and time passing mean something different.

I look upon myself—clear pool of water.
I splash my face and see age,
Not your grey hair but mine.
Astonished heart lets forth bewildered tears.
I did not want change.
I was not happy then—
My sadness now is no surprise.
Age has spun its wicked web.
Time has played its dutiful role.

All this happened to you and me—
Past and future memories
All under the spell of time.
Now the puzzle is solved:
I see you in me.
I am the same,
You are the same—
A paradigm both old and predictable.
Friend is who you are,
Friend is who I am.
Age has not separated us—
Life has made us more interesting.

Don't cast me aside, for I envelop you.
Youth is forever
Time is change
Age is welcome.

Our challenge is to mix this trio.
Hold my hand.
Count my fingers.
Your golden hair,
Thundering sky—
This is all discovery.
Life is unpredictable—
Don't disappoint me.
Live long, age well,
For that is what I wish to do.

10 June 2002
Paris

DUET

Très Bon:
The life in me is joyous.
Seeing people on the streets—
Energy and movement—
Seeing you, seeing all beings,
Happiness is what I see.

La Vie:
You do not understand.
When you walk you see nothing,
Simply the outer appearance.
Do not joke and humor yourself,
For everything in your view
Is tinted, stained by the concepts of happiness and good will.
All are suffering.
In fact, wherever you go,
You, Très Bon,
You think you see goodness
But it is simply me,
Disguised.

Très Bon:
I am shocked!
You of all beings should know:
Yes, beings do suffer;
That is only a transition
Between good and good.
Energy is everywhere,
Joy is the love.
Everyone encounters this.
Do not isolate yourself—
Come with me.

La Vie:
Thinking and seeing,
I reflect—
I have joy
And you are correct:
There are moments
Of pure freedom,
No inhibition,
No embarrassment.
Is this what you mean?

Très Bon:
At times, my friend La Vie,
That's how it may be.
Don't misjudge me—
Sadness makes joy.
Don't corner me—
Love me.
Who am I?
What does it mean to be alive?
Before
Pain and suffering were my fingers
My heart
My day and night.
I was lost.
How could this be joy?

La Vie:
At times you are right, Très Bon,
At others I am right.
La Vie—this is the flow.
You and I must melt

And look beyond,
For life and goodness is both.
The mingling of our thoughts makes
   others.
The honey we produce is genuine—
Beyond conflict, beyond beauty.

Très Bon:
Yes!
Now I feel you, Life.
La Vie, we are not different,
We are not the same,
But we can sit at the same table.

La Vie:
Why oh why
Did you not say this before?

Très Bon:
You never asked!

La Vie:
I always asked,
But could not bear to listen.

Très Bon:
Now you can listen
And all is well.

10 June 2002
Paris

BLUE PLANET

Within my mind I live on a small blue planet.
Everyone seems far away.
Everywhere is blackness,
Yet abundant life consumes each moment.
I wish everyone could see this blue fragile life
Floating in the blackness—
Next time they miss the bus,
Next time they forget to look and smile.

We float on a blue dot—
We should all be frightfully concerned.
No matter what you think, what I think,
We will always be on this blue dot,
Unless you are the master of darkness
Or the emperor of blackness.

Look at each other—
Be kind
Stop
Look up
See blue.
Realize that color came from somewhere.
It could be another color if we don't play our cards right.
We should hold our worst enemies,
Because even they love blue.

10 June 2002
Paris

MEADOWS IN HEAVEN
(For Jeff Rosen)

The moon shines bright, half full of cheese—
Not soy, but genuine butter of the earth.
The other half, full of heart—
Not soy, but living blood, the flesh of humans.
This is Jeff:
Brother, indispensable servant, mutual lover of passion.

Serenity and seriousness is how we pass the time.
His face is stone.
Truth be told,
Bubbling excitement in adolescent frivolity
Is how we spend our time.
Structure and discipline is his nose,
His face is teddy bear and sugar cane.

Day after day, month after month,
We can watch nothing and love each other's company.
Year after year, we have woven this web.
Passion occasionally arises in our conversation.
When it does, a glimmer in our eyes,
We know the love of friendship.

So deep-rooted is our symbiotic dilemma
That others think it's another planet.
This genuine experience of friendship
Has never missed a beat.
When he loves me, I don't care,
And when I love him,
He cares, but doesn't show it.

In this way, the balance is tipped in my favor.
I never abuse it, for he is a recipient, like a meadow in heaven—
Even the gods couldn't fill it.
I am the flower, perpetual spring.
He loves just to watch me—
Not to grab and pluck me from my ground,
But to enjoy me where I am.

Some days, my petals are bright—
Others, they are weary.
Whatever the case may be,
He breathes, he wakes up,
He realizes I am his beauty,
And I know he is mine.

1 July 2002
Halifax, Nova Scotia

FORTUNATE BIRTH

In the kingdom of children
Every one of you is this child:
An innocent being within the womb
Who jumped out of heaven
And landed in Shambhala.
Fortunate birth is who you are.
Everything is perfect in your world.

Your clothing the breath of heaven,
Your feet covered by dragon's mist,
You are the most fortunate beings on earth,
The children of dharma.
Other children suffer and are caught in perpetual dilemma.
Because Buddha has touched you,
You are fortunate.
You are open heart.

Be dharmic now,
Be powerful now,
Be benevolent now—
Not for me, not for others,
But because that is your blood.
When you feel privileged, use it.
When you feel ashamed, pounce.
Consume that hesitation—
It's only a flicker of your imagination.

You are the blessed people on this earth.
Every atom of your being is Buddha—
What's left is joy.

You have no excuse—don't sulk.
You can be sad, for sadness is the most genuine expression.
Expression of goodness is who you are.

Being a child of dharma is dilemma.
Being a child of dharma is freedom.
Consume this hesitation of not knowing.
Never doubt—only walk forward.
Love everything
For that is why you are here.

1 July 2002
Halifax, Nova Scotia

DESPERATE

Desperate to touch a light,
I stretch—
Pain brings me back.
I am consumed by escape,
But everything I touch is full of pain.

I cannot hold a conscious thought.

Then I catch a glimmer in your eyes,
A spark within your smile.
You are sunshine in the morning.
I feel so good, I want to hold you—
Your beaming light rays
So low, so high.

In one moment, I was so there.

Have I escaped the castle of self-love?
Have I liberated myself from the dungeon of pain?
The aching in my heart is gone.
I feel better about me,
Knowing I have room for you.

This is what life is about:
Thinking of you.
When I do that, I am universal,
When I do that, I am personal,
When I do that, I am me.
I am so volatile—life is so volatile:
One moment, pain—
The next, love.
In this journey,
Can I learn from both?

8 July 2002
Boulder, Colorado

78

VAJRA FAREWELL

Listening to the wind,
I hear the dharma of great bliss wisdom.
I am a wandering yogin.
The winds of the past have brought me here.
The fire of now illuminates the future.

Knowing how to listen
Has revealed the depth, the bodhi-mind.
As air passes through my body,
I open to universal wonderment.
My mind naturally relaxes because I am free to move,
Not tethered to one spot or harnessed to another,
No longer a kite, duality pulling my string.

As I drink the self-arising brook,
Each sip melds samsara and nirvana.
Before
Pleasure and pain
Good and bad
Were my guiding winds.
Now wisdom's release glows
In the sail of basic goodness—pure and perfect.
That is the mind—that is the world:
Honey dripping from a flower in space,
Landing on this sacred earth.
My journey now is to keep moving,
To let wisdom's winds guide me
Across this sweet earth.

5 August 2002
Shambhala Mountain Center

COME, COME, AND DANCE

The buddhas take me by my hand
And whisper in my ear:
Come, come, and dance.

New and old friends
Tell me they want to be near.
I tell them I never went anywhere.
The buddhas say come, come, and dance.

My mother and father say they love me;
I ask them why they have to tell me this.
The buddhas say come, come, and dance.

When the world tries to teach me,
Dishes fall and rainbows appear.
Some people give me things and others take them away.
The buddhas say come, come, and dance.

Each morning I want to be brave, fearless,
Help everyone I see.
But this summer day turns to rain.
The buddhas say come, come, and dance.

When I gather strength,
I can hold the whole universe in my heart.
I become brother and sister, mother and father,
And the buddhas take my hand.
They say come, come, and dance.

High in the sky in their secret place,
They tell me to look at others.

I never thought it could be so simple.
This is a secret to be shared.
Come, come with me.

Let's look into everyone's heart,
Look through their eyes.
It's all about joy and helping others.
Come, come, and dance.

8 August 2002
Shambhala Mountain Center

RADIATING MIND

Radiating mind, perceptions crisp and clear—
How many beings live in this space?
Stretching mind, expanding concepts,
Can this fresh openness envelop the earth?
Cape of space invites me to come forth,
Mingle and dance, wrap it around me,
Jump in and play without boundaries.
That is what my heart yearns to do.
Floating toward the heavens
My body is weightless; my mind, grounded.
This space peels my skin of inhibition—
Hesitation drips like water from feathers.
Flying and sitting are the same.

I am buoyant
Swimming
Free from the friction of gravity
Gliding beyond the boundaries I held.
My courage to explore has opened this dimension of liquid joy.
Thinking I would move from here to there, from in to out,
I loosened
Relaxed
Trusted inner strength
And fell from riding the creature of concept.
When I landed, having given up accomplishment
I saw the universe in my heart.

Now I have crossed the threshold between what is known
And not known.
This space doesn't care if I go further or come near.

I have transcended who I thought I was
And am
And will be.
What mattered before is irrelevant.
What seemed momumental is insignificant.
Even time sits on my lap, a small pet that I stroke.
Concepts are like this creature making noise for attention.
This is the sphere of naked truth:
Unchanging, unwavering dharmakaya.

8 August 2002
Shambhala Mountain Center

A SEED WAITING TO GROW

This summer lasted forever—
Stories of heat told time.
When we met, you were looking for love,
Wanting to offer a heart of jewels.
You were a seed waiting to grow.

You'd forgotten to look at the sky;
You fell down to rest in my hand.
I loved you with thunder and rain,
With the raging fire of my heart.
You were a seed waiting to grow.

These mountains of hope that we climb
Help me to show you the sky.
We see that fear is as empty as air
And now the seed can grow.

Jump from now and fly with me—
Catch the dragon of summer joy.
Burn your fear in wisdom's fire—
Dissolve it in tomorrow's dawn.
The jewel that rises is you and me.

Walk with me in heaven's meadow—
Let's be free from hope and fear.
Release the birds of happiness,
Let swim the fish of love.
When our hearts touch, the golden earth smiles.
You are a flower in full bloom.

8 August 2002
Shambhala Mountain Center

LADIES AND GENTLEMEN

Some men try,
Others try harder.
Some women say,
"Why do you try at all?"

Some men wish,
Others wish harder.
Some women say,
"Do you wish for me, or for you?"

Some men leave,
Others never come home.
Some women say,
"Why do you go? Do you need to come back?"

Then all the men gather together and say,
"We are here for a reason.
Do you not see our value—
Why we try so hard and wish so much?"

And the women say,
"For us you do not have to try, go away, or wish so much.
All that effort—trying and wishing—
Maybe it's for you and you alone.
We want you to be close.
Don't go far away.

"For we hold the hearth, and you the flame.
Nature's law, we understand, makes you burn;
Flames take you far away.
Don't transcend the earth that gave you birth
But stay, for we await you.

"Are you space, thinking you are earth,
And we are sky, thinking we are earth,
Ground solid, untransformed?
Between the two, we have a child who has a home.
Now we must learn.
You need to be earth, we need to be sky,
Both looking up and down.
That is where love and life rest."

16 August 2002
Bell Bay, Cape Breton

PERFECT SWING

Sunshine beckons.
A leaf floats high in the sky,
Turning and rotating,
Gold and red.
My heart glistens.

We Shambhala golfers
Take delight in the purity of white.
"Beyond hesitation" is our motto.
With a warrior's confidence,
Our bodies move like the wind,
Our minds like a pouncing tiger,
Still but strong.

The heat of middle earth has come upon
This mesmerizing island of Cape Breton.
Upon this Gaelic land we sweat,
Drip with love and affection.
Resonating as a foursome—
That is natural geomancy.
Teeing it high or teeing it low—
That is every man's dilemma.
Hole in one or hole in many?

Our minds do not waver,
For we know the seasons.
Wind, rain, or sun—
In our hearts, these dralas never depart.
They stay to test our humor.
The point is never to finish
But always to be on the path.

This concoction teaches us that life is virtuous,
Speckled with moments of frustration.
Taking the horizon, the sky, as our guide,
Let's swing away without fear or hope.

16 August 2002
Bell Bay, Cape Breton

JUMP START

We wrap our hands around this little rosary so tightly,
Gripping each bead,
Wondering where it will take us—
Good or bad?

What fate will befall us as we cling to prayer and religion?
Life is vast, but we reduce it to chance and superstition:
The color we wear predicts our luck,
Our favorite shirt defines our success,
Our unlucky belt determines failure.

Creatures of science, we pride ourselves on asking,
"Have we made any progress?"
Whether or not these technologies help us,
Ultimately we rely on Mother Luck,
A string of beads of inconsistent size.

Fate is not determined by inevitability
But by wishing really, really hard.
And when our dream happens,
We kiss our rosary and thank the gods.

16 August 2002
Bell Bay, Cape Breton

ISLAND PROCLAMATION

Thundering time rolls through this land.
The ancient lore says parts are African—others Welsh and
   Gaelic.
These hills like perfect wood
Construct an altar to the heavens
And wait for gods to land,
Surrounded by great ocean—
Unknown drala blue enveloping this isle with mirth and gleam.

Depression and suppression grip these islanders.
Do not surrender—fight,
Knowing you are children of heaven and ocean.
Not in a million years could anyone have the luck
To be born of such parents.

Don't abuse each other
But take this natural beauty—
Accept yourselves as chosen.
Dance to the Celtic music.
Don't sing to your demise!

You will win because you are good—
And they are not bad.
They suffer because they have too many.
You have everything—
Keep it simple.
Exhale your victory!
Your love transcends a thousand aeons:
Everything always wins over many.

16 August 2002
Bell Bay, Cape Breton

DRALAS ON YOUR SHOULDERS
(For David Mukpo)

Seventeen summers ago the news came:
Yung-lo David was born into the Mukpo clan.
I took this message to the Dorje Dradül;
Hence he asked me to announce it to the troops.
This ground of Magyal Pomra is your birthright.
It was karmic coincidence that brought you here.

Emperor Yung-lo was forefather to the kingdom of Shambhala.
His yellow wisdom guided many beings on the path of dharma.
Being a warrior, he conquered his fears.
Being a bodhisattva, he opened his heart to all.

Growing up in this unpredictable world
Is challenging—day-to-day, moment-to-moment.
Now you, David of Mukpo,
Are passing through the gates of youth to manhood.
As the dralas land on your shoulders
May you gain inspiration, conquer your aggression,
Vanquish your desires, and burn your ignorance.

Take your seat in this mandala of the Great Eastern Sun.
Let the sun shine from your heart.
Be like the ancestral sovereign of China and Shambhala—
Yung-lo, a general and king:
Lead others to the mountain of liberation.
That is your heritage.
Three cheers for the birth of David Mukpo!

20 August 2002
Tatamagouche, Nova Scotia

MAGYAL POMRA

Little dreams are created with big ideas.
You are little beings with big ideas.
Your being is so big
Even Zeus can't hold you in his hands;
Your heart so bountiful
Even Chenrezig has to breathe when you enter the room.
Your exertion is so monumental
That Achilles reaches out trying to do more.
Your joy envelops Vajrapani:
His mantra of power surrounds you.
Kasung of enjoyment,
The flower of Dionysus lands in your hand.
Yeshe Tsogyal is your lover,
The kasung Gesar is your eyes—
Gazing, staring, knowing everything is possible.
Denma beats the drum,
Your bloodflow dependent on his heartbeat.

We are so Mukpo!
We are so Great Eastern Sun!
We are so basic goodness!
We are Poseidon with trident,
Surrounded by the ocean of the worlds.
This is Magyal Pomra.

20 August 2002
Magyal Pomra Encampment
Tatamagouche, Nova Scotia

SWORD IN HAND
(For Norrie Wright)

As I swing through life
It teaches me to see illusion,
To look at others, see the brightness in their eyes
And keep compassion as my motto.
Everything we do is universal if we do it right.

These lessons where I learn to swing through time and space
Connect me to heritage, tradition, and the mystic.
As I take this sword in hand
I learn to cut hesitation and disbelief.
When I strike the final blow,
Heaven, earth, and man unite.

This transmission comes to me as gentle breeze and thunderbolt—
The legendary voice of golf, Norrie,
Whose utterance of wisdom says
That there are many ways to swing through life
But ultimately only one—the Tao.
In his heart he knows the way.
Whether or not he reveals it depends on karmic conditions.

The master of energy shows me how to bring life into my weapon.
Let the Florida sun help us keep our hope alive.
The gentle breeze at Neptune Beach
Reminds us to inhale gratitude, to feel fortunate,
For others walk through life looking down.
We have been given the gift of how to swing,
Always looking up.

16 February 2003
Jacksonville, Florida

THOUGHTS

Thinking, thinking, thinking.
So many thoughts!
Haven't finished one thought—
Another one is born, demanding my attention.
Where are these thoughts coming from?
Bubbles in the mud, they pop when touched by air.

Why am I constantly surrounded by thoughts?
Are they friend or foe, enemy or ally?
Whose mind is this, anyway?
If it were my mind,
I could say
"Stop, don't worry"
And it would happen
Just like magic.

I have this magic,
My magic,
The magic that happens when my mind is an ally.
Within this mind
I know there is peace and strength—
Synchronicity innate, unwavering potential.

I just have to see that I'm thinking too much.
Past and future is where I dwell.
Here for a moment
I dart off to the future,
Worrying about what could happen.
Then I'm terrorized by the past,
Remembering what could go wrong.
I am missing my life, my very own life.

I must take a stand,
Make friends with this wildness.
This wild horse will take me to freedom,
The open expanse, new horizon.

First I must breathe—
Exhale inhibitions
Inhale the present moment
Exhale thoughts of past and future.
Breathing brings wisdom,
Freedom from fantasizing.

Now I feel the breath of the horse.
I offer a morsel of food—
Sweet grain of nowness
This horse enjoys.

I place the saddle of strength on its back,
The bridle on its majestic head.
The shiny silver bit
Expresses clarity of mind.

Relaxed and confident—
Horse and rider have mutual love.
The window opens.
Green fields invite me.
The horse takes a leap—
I am free.

24 February 2003
Seabright, N.S.

PEACE

What is peace?
Peace of mind, peace of heart, world peace?
Where is it?
In heaven, earth, or human?

Contemplating peace,
I see harmony, no more struggle, free from suffering.
I don't see peace in many places,
Just friction, anger—paths to pain.

Suffering is a fervent attempt toward peace—
Peace at any cost.
The search for peace becomes so one-pointed,
We create suffering for all.

The challenge of true peace—
Not angry peace or jealous peace,
But peace free from desperation—
Is to create harmony of body, speech, and mind.
Can we make harmony?
Peace means putting patience before anger.

Be at peace.
Then life will change from suffering to joy—
Joy to bring peace.
We must be strong before demanding strength of others.

I'll continue to think about peace
But now I'm going to sit in peace.
Come join me.

23 February 2003
Seabright, N.S.

96

THE SUN WILL SHINE

Snow falls on my hand.
Under my gaze, it melts,
Soaks deep into my heart.
I feel cold, alone.
Everything I touch is cold, alone.
Tears land on my skin—cold, alone.
Is life this way for everyone?

Yet my heart tells me
It's alive, I'm alive.
Through its pulse,
Rhythm of a new life,
I hear, "Notice me. Use me.
I can grow big enough to touch others.
You are alive!
You have heat!
A tremendous fire burns in you—
Set   it   free!"

Eyes water as sunlight bounces off my cheek.
The tears feel the heat like snowflakes.
This magical heart warms my being.

I look at you, touch you—
Your heart too begins to beat.
Our mutual radiance comes to life.
Frigidity is melting—
Earth begins to warm.
We are not meant to be alone and cold.
As faint as it may be, listen to the warm beat.
Then the sun will shine.

25 February 2003
Seabright, N.S.

THE MOON

The moon, the moon—
I hear so much about the moon,
But when I see the moon resting
On my hand, on my heart,
I say, "This moon is so beautiful—
I feel uncontrollable hope that all beings can love each other
Like the moon loves itself."

When I feel the moon in my hands,
It is the most beautiful of gems.
It glows, and all I can dream
Is that all beings hold the moon in their hearts
And let life's cool breeze blow.
If it blows, life is love.
If it doesn't, this beautiful moon cannot shine.

Who is to blame?
I wish I could take all the blame into my heart
And make it the moon itself.
Then all hesitation could simply be the blossoming of the moon.

Live, dance, and play—
That is what the moon does.
Look into the water and see the beauty
Of a clear circle that reflects the best of life.
This life is you and me.
This moon is you and me.
We are the moon—the moon is who we are.
I love who we are.
I love being the moon.

FEELING
(For three-year retreatants)

Within an emotional mind
Feelings constantly change.
Gazing at a teacup
Hearing the sound of traffic
Sitting cross-legged in a desolate desert free of distraction—
How do I feel?

On the horizon a lonesome traveler,
A silhouette separate from time and space,
Pulled along by feelings.
Gaze at a lover—feel delight.
Look at the world—feel pain.
Recall the snow lion—feel tingling spine,
Life-force energy.

Feeling is a strange thing:
We cannot say dharmata is feelingless.
We cannot separate our understanding—
Unshakable realization—
From feeling.
That would contradict the natural laws of great perfection.
For milk is both wholesome and sweet
Love is eternal and fleeting
Devotion is mundane and sublime.

Those who walk this meditative land
Must relax into the ebb and flow of feeling.
How can we freeze heat?
Don't separate morning and evening,
Now and then.
But be careful:

Don't weave them into a blanket
And fall asleep.
Just be awake, always awake,
Then you will feel better.

27 March 2003
Chicago, Illinois

ADVENTURE GREAT EASTERN SUN

Busyness
Agitation
Aggression—
Are these convenience?
Electricity makes more work—
Does it illuminate our minds?

Here illumination arises as desert sun—
Hot, scorching, and merciless—
With its dancing partner Green River,
Mother of fertile possibility.

This river of bodhichitta
Refreshes us,
Renews our senses.
Loving kindness dripping with compassion
Brings down aggression's tallest buttes.

We think we are real,
But when we swim in Green River,
The current of wakefulness
Swallows us.

Panic!
Where does this river lead?
All the way to wisdom.

29 May 2003
Green River, Utah

TIMING

A swallow in the sky
Told me I was happy.
I ducked my head
Into the water—
Pure blue and deep,
So refreshing I could barely hold myself in my skin.

Love told me I was happy.
Running, I ran.
I could not stop running.
A distant mountain looked unreachable and monumental,
But my little feet, one after the other,
Made that mountain my friend.
It came running to me.

I love sunshine.
When I see it, I feel powerful.
Gazing into sky,
My eyes part the clouds
And I bask in the power of radiance.
That is why I am so happy.

Don't lose your gift—
Everybody has one.
Maybe it's the sun or the moon,
A lucky belt.
Everybody has a moment
When they're happy.

Why?
Because we are all meant to be happy.

If you think I am full of yak, horse, or bull,
Then look at yourself in the mirror.
Don't you want to be happy?
Everyone else is just like you.
I'm happy.

21 June 2003
Halifax, Nova Scotia

MIDSUMMER'S DAY

Leaning back
I stretch my arms.
Falling, descending,
I could encompass the whole horizon wnd hold it on my
    chest—
Warmth, sunshine, humidity.
The tattoo of life displays itself:
Poppies, peonies,
Rhododendrons, sunflowers, daisies,
Foliage, blades of grass.
This is summer, a miracle we thought could never happen.

When I dance in my mind,
Summer is my mood.
When I wash my hands,
Summer is the season.
When I taste the salt in my sweat,
Summer is a blessing—warmth, incredible heat.
Don't be shy:
Everything is a season full of potential.

Why do we love summer?
Because it is the season of love.
Every summer the summer of love,
The summer that all hold in their hearts.
Let that warmth be free.
When it encompasses the whole world,
That is summer—
The summer we all meet,
The summer we all wake up
And realize life is wonderful.

21 June 2003
Halifax, Nova Scotia

104

THINK TWICE AND BE HAPPY

Trees
Sky
Moon
Clouds—
All are descending.
The sky grey,
Inspiration placid,
Even my words dull.
Hail and snow would be a gift:
Rain might allow me to drown.
I feel so down
Not even miners with their helmets
Would encounter me at this depth;
I do not joke and play with upbeat verses.

I was born a true free spirit,
Was once a young man
Who knew heaven was high and earth was good.
I loved a woman and she loved me—
I kissed her and she smiled.
I hugged and held her close.
I saw myself wanting to be loved and scared,
But now I have nowhere to go.
Everything is shriveled up, closed in.

Like a mountain lion scratching the earth,
Hoping to find a trace of life, I dig—
Not in the earth, but in my heart.
Amazing!
I cannot believe that here within
Lies buried such goodness
Yearning

Courage
Compassion
Intelligence
Hopefulness
Humor—
A brook bubbling through the Grand Canyon
Traffic in Manhattan
Lakeside wind in Chicago.
Life was always in me—
Now I am the source of light
I looked for everywhere.

21 June 2003
Halifax, Nova Scotia

THREE SORBETS

Speed

Touching my heart
I collapse.
I must make the green light.
I'm not driving a car.

Funny

I wanted to catch my breath.
Everyone was laughing.
I died.

Stupid

I thought I told you
But I guess someone forgot.
Life—that's the hard part.

21 June 2003
Halifax, Nova Scotia

GOODBYE

Goodbye.
That's my practice
Morning, afternoon, evening.
"Hello," is what I say
But in reality, I am saying goodbye.

Life is a continuum,
A practice of saying goodbye:
Sometimes a little goodbye
Sometimes a big goodbye
Sometimes a casual, nonchalant goodbye.

We're always fooling ourselves,
Covering up the goodbye with a hello.
Hello to my face in the mirror when I wash early in the morning
Hello to my socks and shoes
Hello to the road I walk on, the sky I gaze into.
Constantly I yearn and fool myself
With "hello."

If I am truly fearless and courageous
I will realize the nature of goodbye.
It's okay to say goodbye.
Goodbyes make the best of friends.
Goodbyes give us dignity—
Freedom from holding on so tight,
Ignoring the inevitable.
When I meet somebody for the first time,
I can say goodbye,
For truly that is how friendship will end.
Next time I drink coffee, I will say goodbye.

As I breathe in the sunshine on Midsummer's Day,
I feel liberated because I can say goodbye,
Knowing it is good—it is very, very good.
Life is a perpetual release,
A lesson that the cosmos says goodbye.

This song was sung by a traveler
Who delights in knowing how to say goodbye.

22 June 2003
Dorje Denma Ling

HAPPINESS HA HA

When I dunk my head,
Grabbing an apple in deep water,
Everybody laughs.
I find it crisp, refreshing.
The goal of such frivolity in summer heat
Seems worthwhile.
I would sacrifice myself for this
Intensely inconsequential but enjoyable endeavor.
Life is full of these predicaments—
Meaning to me,
Recreation to others.

To Hollywood tycoons
Wall Street financiers
Or street sweepers,
Such moments are the epitome of life—
All it has to offer.
All we have are our moments of escape:
Humorous escapades
Sexual dalliances
Athletic obsessions.
Apart from this,
We are all but the end of a joke.
No one knows who started it,
But we're not ready to laugh at the punch line.

We think we're free and imaginative.
We think we're risky and adventurous.
But now let's really laugh—
Let's laugh at everybody.
Smile inside at ourselves

And make that leap into cosmic superstardom
Where we can liberate our minds.

That is the star of the future,
The one that everyone will follow—
Empty of jealousy, arrogance, and pride,
Full of the moon of compassion
And the sun of wisdom.

22 June 2003
Halifax, Nova Scotia

GLIMPSE OF NATURE

A little blackbird
Flew across my mind and landed on my head.
When it cried, I thought the whole world was shaking.
I looked up and saw sunflowers coming out of the sky,
Looked down and saw rainbow fishes
In the blue, deep blue, very deep blue water.

The ocean grabbed me and water splashed up,
Kissed my cheeks—I knew it loved me.
When I looked around, I was shocked,
For no one was there.

My heart jumped into my palm.
Why was it so red?
I wanted to say thanks
But it burped and smiled
And disappeared!—
Back into my chasm of a body.

Like a child surprised at life happening so fast,
Unable to order or direct it,
All I could remember was
Sitting on a fence post
Minding my business
Hoping to catch a glimpse of nature
Secretly wishing I could find myself,
When this little world that no one will ever see
Showed me everything.

25 June 2003
Halifax, Nova Scotia

THE QUANDARY

I thought I left myself—
I wanted to escape.
But I mustn't have gotten very far:
Everywhere looked very familiar.
Either I didn't recognize myself
Or I knew very little about myself.
Either way, my attempt to part
Left me in a quandary.

Is it possible to leave anywhere?
Once we know, once we see,
Can we leave?
I was hoping to leave,
Wishing to leave,
But Mother Nature jumped out,
Smacked me and said,
"You're not going anywhere."

How I wish I could go and come freely.
But in reality even freedom comes
At the expectation of entrapment.
Don't try to jump.

All the little birds will not fly away.
Be unpredictable and realize
No one knows who's running and who's scared.
We are all wanting, but without hope.

26 June 2003
Halifax, Nova Scotia

SECRET

When I keep a secret
No one ever knows.
When someone tells me something
I won't ever think about it again,
Unless the sun, the wind, or a beautiful day
Looks at me and says,
"Well, what do you know?
What are you holding so tight?"
Then I can only say what is true,
What I've kept buried.
All the secrets—small and large—
Come gushing out.

If someone sees me telling the secrets,
It's like a river of birds coming from my heart,
A stream of butterflies coming from my lips,
All the secrets coming out, fluttering around,
Touching the person I'm with:
These truths
Land between their eyes
Penetrate their heart
Melt into their pupils
And fly up their nose.
They think, "Wow—truly wow—
How lucky I am to breathe in, to hear such delight.
This is truly a secret no one should ever know."

The climate this creates in people cannot be fathomed.
The intimacy and directness of secrets that bind human beings
Cannot be fully understood.

These utterances,
Relationships woven by word and breath,
Have some cosmic value, some heavenly connotation.
Why?
Because it is the nature of mind and heart that is secret.
Why else would secrecy be so important?

Don't doubt, catch, or hold me—
I am beyond ransom.
That's how profound these truths are.

Be a rebel and spin on your head,
Come out dizzy and smile.
Reveal nothing to anyone
Unless you see his head spinning, too.
Then you can say,
"You look like you have a secret."

If he smiles, turn around and around and around—
He is guaranteed to be your friend.
How else could you know
When something is secret and worth keeping secret?
When you finally stop spinning, he looks at you and says
Nothing.

26 June 2003
Halifax, Nova Scotia

STEAMBOAT SPRINGS

Hot life can cook us.
Very hot life can test us.
Unbearable hot life would be good.

We've seen this paradox.
When I sweat, a giant washcloth is my umbrella.
The pain of overwhelming warmth
Brings visions of Kilimanjaro's cool waters
Descending like snowflakes of hope.
Tongue catches them—
They soak into my skin.

Heat
Hot
Very hot.
The mind is very hot.
Nothing is as hot or direct as the mind.
What is this vapor—wisdom?
The sun is wisdom.
Simply not knowing what to do is wisdom.
Tying shoelaces, kissing a friend is wisdom.
Seeing projection is wisdom.
I jump from great height to show you this wisdom.
Please look up occasionally
And see that wisdom is always above you.
It looks like the sun in the sky.

14 July 2003
Steamboat Springs, Colorado

ON THE SPOT

Cosmic liberation of beings occurred on this little trip from home.
Expectations as placid as the waves of Prince Edward Island
Were crushed by Mount Everest of profound joy.
When tantalizing and scintillating intelligence grabs hold of
     humanity,
A classic truth that can only be expressed by unequivocal joy must
     be proclaimed.
This is equanimity.

Everybody and everything needs to be put on the spot—
It is my duty to find which spot and which time.
With these lovers of truth and honey-soaked joy
I have chosen PEI as the fulcrum of all intentions, wishes, and
     purposes.

This little red earth,
Little red island,
Is the wish-fulfilling jewel.
When we come here, we purify and celebrate.
This is true glory:
Knowing that truth is within
And proclaiming Shambhala as sociable.*

*"Sociable" is the word that Islanders shout when they are toasting together.

13 August 2003
Charlottetown, Prince Edward Island

HIGH-FIDELITY LOVE

Are you ready for a little co-emergent bliss?
Are your engines filled with love of dharma
Ready to propel you?
This is heavy metal truth
Good taste
Fuel for the all-consuming mind
That wants to be hip.

Bad-ass music makes me cry.
Don't all beings have goodness as the basis?
Why do we torture ourselves this way?
Must the cornucopia of high fidelity be megawatted
Until we can't feel our numbness?
Is it prosperity or suckiness—
Its failure to express itself—
Especially in the realm of love?

Is what we want and somehow miss
High-fidelity love?
Is how they got their love-fix all that separates
Mozart
Eric Clapton
Marvin Gaye
Willie Nelson
Sting
Godsmack
Norah Jones
Milarepa
And Longchenpa?
What if all the beings in the world

At the wrong time in the wrong place
Just didn't hear someone say, "I love you"?
Did that moment create this ensemble of music
Varied and heartfelt
All at the root full of love?

13 August 2003
Charlottetown, Prince Edward Island

MY FRIEND BARRY BOYCE

Proxy or proximo?
Total confusion or confused?
Sanitarium or sanity?
Jovial or joker?
I believe all of these words describe my friend Dapön Barry Boyce.

P.S.: Is he
Friend or faithful?
Idiot or idiotic?
Fearful or fearless?
Fat or feastful?
These words too describe my friend Barry Boyce.

But at times I wonder,
Freakish or futuristic?
Happy or hilarious?
Paternal or paranoid?
Barry Boyce, or some of these words?

But you must know
He is uncontrollably a whimsical adolescent
Who perpetually pretends to project
Pessimistic parlays and diabolical infractions
Upon an endemic deteriorated deviant delusional
Dot dot dot
Dharmic individual.

From a happy, healed habitué of the human realm
Who is hilariously thankful that humor is his heart's blood.

13 August 2003
Charlottetown, Prince Edward Island

MARS IS HOT

Why are we here?
Mars is hot
I feel freakish
The Buddha is red
Now is our time.

Enlightenment has never been so close—
Jump at the chance.
Don't be a fool and think you have to be mean.
What a pendulum!
Action is no joke
And life should be sober,
Especially when we are dancing on the edge of sanity.

Take a break and kiss fortune!
Tell her that we jump at magic
And then fall away
Into a deep blue ocean,
Knowing that if we drown
We drown in wisdom.

13 August 2003
Charlottetown, Prince Edward Island

HAPPY BIRTHDAY MR. PRESIDENT!
(For Richard Reoch)

In the garden of Shambhala
There arose a massive tree.
This beautiful display of nature
Was the most precious wish of the Rigdens.
When the silken breeze that radiated from the queen mother of
    basic goodness
Blew upon this tree,
All beings dissolved into an undeniable joy.
Some danced, others sang songs.
This tree of Ashe has been placed by an absolute command of the
    benevolent Sakyong:
"The realm of peace and happiness must be provided for all who
    toil in the suffering of confusion."

But this is a happy day!
In fact this is a happy birthday day!
We celebrate this day
Where the burial mound of Richard the Lion Heart lay;
Now the birthday of Richard the Terrifying Face is born,
Bringing cheer and happiness.
Since his chi is strong like the wish-fulfilling tree of Shambhala,
He is the master of many hearts and time zones.
Even the kryptonite of wheat does not cause his remaining hairs
    to stand up.
Since there are five buddhas and five skandhas,
Five ways of raising windhorse,
Five paths towards ultimate enlightenment,
I cheerfully celebrate your fifty-fifth birthday!
Knowing that your roots are deep, I send many blessings as you
    reach into the heavens.

23 August 2003
Dechen Chöling

BLUE, ALWAYS

As dütsi drops into the mind of the sky dancer
Known as Indestructable Joy,
The reality of the common path dawns.

We speak the language of samsara.
Eh Ma!
Dissolve communication.
Let nature speak—
For when it does,
It is unbiased and pure.

On the staircase of hope and fear
We are too happy to utter the words real and unreal.
Let us release these words into the sky,
Clear and unfabricated.
When we finally let go,
We will fall back in utter relaxation and realize
It was always blue.

29 August 2003
Dechen Chöling

THE HORIZON

When the snow lion of absolute power roars,
It proclaims the beautiful flower
Known in the three times
As pure passion and hesitation.

The dandelions of Wyoming,
The cosmic winds of Kansas,
Elevate my chin
So I can blow a kiss
Across the horizon.
When they receive it,
Warriors hold their saddles, spur the wind.
Then timeless change gallops
On the horizon.

Don't doubt our warrior tradition.
I am the embodiment of power and wisdom.
KI! SO!
Everyone is a warrior.
Don't catch me looking at you asleep.

30 August 2003
Dechen Chöling

BIRD'S EYE VIEW

Pheasants and phoenixes play with chickens—
What foul weather this mind of duality can produce!
If only I could kick myself,
Not from self-loathing or anger,
But simply to jump-start the chicken in my heart.

If we could accept what nature has provided,
Continual complaint might exhaust itself at last.
These climatic changes in mind and heart are never ending.
We are own weather people—
Every five minutes we need a new forecast.

We need a garuda typhoon,
To be tossed and twirled,
To realize the unnecessary chatter,
Rest in the middle of that storm,
And let the peaceful eye of wisdom
Blow concepts from our heads.

When the merciless garuda of carefree wisdom swallows us whole,
Encapsulates us in the perfect egg of unfathomable space,
We're able to relax.
If you ask me then, "How's the weather?"
I'll say, "It's basically good."

8 September 2003
Dechen Chöling

CULMINATION

The energy of winter has produced a supreme sunburst.
A child expands its arms as far as the universe.
This inconceivable awakening takes place
In the self-existing land of great bliss,
Meadows that cover samsara and nirvana,
Where cows graze with vajralike ignorance.

This summer we offered token habitual pattern.
Out of nowhere we took refuge in this very moment,
A brief and utterly surprising confluence
Of past and present,
Future and nowhere,
Reveling now in the mirror of my hand.

Spring forth, unwanted hesitation!
Let this meandering inability to make a decision be pickled
    mercilessly.
When tears come, the future will be reflected in each drop.
Taste it.
Let the salt cleanse and make your world taste good.
Falling back is not an option now.
We have discovered a simple truth here:
Mushrooms spring forth out of nowhere
And so has our enlightenment.

The journey of indecision and confidence will play on
    the stage of mind.
It's time now just to laugh.
Smile with a full heart of true inspiration.
If genuineness guides our kite in the sky of not-knowing,

All the seasons will come forth:
Change will seem like a good thing.

This will occur only if we want it to.
Come forth now.
Pick up your pots and pans
Grab that meditation belt
And walk this path.
Look at the face of every single being.
That's where life begins.

8 September 2003
Dechen Chöling

GOLDEN LOTUS

When time tells me a story,
My mind leaps into the future
And hopes it's in the right place.
In this delightful rendezvous of friends,
Some are consumed by the past,
Others by the future,
Some, occasionally, by the present.

I've been delighted with time since birth.
When things began,
I found the end.
When boredom showed its face,
I was terrified.
Now these childish interpretations
Have fallen away like plumage from a white falcon
Disappearing into sun.
That appearance of beginningless and endless
Has brought us to this moment
When I look at you, and you look at me.

You are deep—I know that.
I am deep, and you know that,
But we are lost in the universe of cosmic action.
Everything that infinity touches seems unreal.
Everything I bring forth as a thought of great importance
Becomes a diminished star.

This whirlwind of understanding
Leaves me perplexed.
I thought things went from here to there,

From there to beyond.
I was caught in the hurricane of conceptuality
Looking at my watch.
What time is it?
I have no idea when anything began.
It was all thought.

Now I'm experiencing the end,
Predetermined long ago.
Why?
Because time is the dragon's tail—it has no laws.
In the inscrutable sky it plays.
When it looks at us,
We are struck by expectation,
Not hearing the thunder of freedom.

Let time and space go.
They were never there—
Nothing to lose.
Release the butterfly,
Look at the eyes of time on its wings,
Not to be held.
It's time.

11 September 2003
Dechen Chöling

MAGIC SAID HELLO

Goodness—
When that guppy takes the hook,
Humanity is caught.
That's when love jumps forward
And says, "I have a bite."

The prospects:
Sunshine has passed
Clouds cover 42nd Street
Broadway looks good.
Let the biggest city in the north tame humanity.
That's why I incarnated—
Love of action.

Time—it was my heartbeat.
Now that anger is more popular
Shall we suck its blood?
When Madam Jealousy kisses my elbow,
Amazement takes over—
Is anyone awake?
Big street holds me responsible—
Sunshine strikes.

Let the gods of beauty relax
In true good fortune.
Loving is perpetual surprise,
Not future pastime.
I want to be delighted and I am.
I could run forever,
But magic said hello.

17 September 2003
Altea, Spain

KISS MY HEART
(For Chris and Saskia Tamdjidi)

Little darlings are the descent of heaven.
When everybody wants to say something,
You are the belt buckle—
Tight but provocative.

I want to display myself.
Why hesitate?
Time is the reason—
Is it going to run out?
Will you lick my toes and kiss my heart?
That's a question for the world.

The air nowadays
Says life has changed its course.
You spoke of beauty,
Your heart beautiful to see.
Here's a kiss—
Love and heartfelt wish
For an entire world full of peace,
Free of anguish.
That's how to serve friendship.

Grab my waist—
Right now is all we have.
Jump with me, love.
No one knows me
And now you know.
I've wanted to jump from the beginning
But was too afraid to tell.

Let's fall into the dragon's thunder,
Abandon pettiness,
Relax into the cosmos.
Think I'm being wild?
It's you who's disconnected—
I never left anywhere.

17 September 2003
Altea, Spain

GROUND LUNGTA
(For Deborah Bright and Ben Pressman)

When I asked the warriors
To come sit at my campfire
Under the starry night of Kalapa,
You came.

As the soft glow of prajna
Illuminated your faces,
The flickering motion of concept
Revealed one thing, then another.

As time passed,
Your whole being came to rest in my hand.
I knew then that each flower that was picked,
Each feather that fell,
Was a cosmic language telling us
We were meant to drink from the same stream.

After ten years, has your thirst been quenched?
In the journey of a buddha
It's been a blink of an eye.
However, we are beings who prefer
To walk this rocky landscape—
Its pinecones and tree bark
The texture of our skin.

You are the morning pony of Shambhala.
Summer rain, winter snow—
Even the Stupa will shed a tear or two,
The salt it came from churned by the lovebirds
Shamatha and Vipashyana.

From the hilly mountains of Germany,
The blue skies of Europe,
I send a kiss of gratitude.
May these lips land among the Rockies
And find their way to Benny-Joe and Deborah.

Remember that the Ashe goes where you go.
Compassion is your handkerchief—
Hand it to another when milk is spilt.
Life never happened—
It just seemed like it did.
Tomorrow is the day you'll realize
The present is important.

Mount the windhorse.
Don't look back.
Ride east,
Or maybe in the beginning, a little south.
Find the dawn,
Relax there,
Build a small home made of light.

That's where we'll meet next.

3 October 2003
Heinsheim, Germany

HAGGIS AND BUBBLE AND SQUEAK

Grrreat was this retreat.
In fact it may have been the grrreatest retreat of them all.
I'm not sentimental,
But I might be a wee bit when I leave the Tower.
Here comes my latte.
I can hear the movement of feet.
Is it Sharon's shoes
Or Emily brewing nettle tea?

Wait! Do I see Matt and Gawang trying to escape out the
    front gate, pretending to take a walk?
I'm not sure if I should try to stop them
Or drag what's left of Justin from the sauna.

Look like Ben's still trying to lose weight by eating chocolate.
Unfortunately I got a peek into Jon's diary—
Pages and pages of the same sentence:
"No running makes Jon a big boy."
Occasional abrupt entrance—"I need more ice."

Meanwhile Michael is counting T-bone steaks as he tries to
    fall asleep
Since there are no sheep because we ate them all.
Uh oh!
Everybody hide!
I think Emily wants to play musical rooms again.

Rinpoche has gained and lost the same five pounds
One hundred and eight times.

Wait! I think Sharon wants to make my bed again.
Achthung! Michael has reorganized the teas again
While Peter is in the basement, forging a new driver's license.

Early this morning I got a peek into the cockpit of a low-flying jet.
It was Ben and Ilsa checking to see if we had moved any furniture.
All they could see was Gawang sending desperate e-mails back to
    the monastery—
Something like, "Get me the hell-realm out of here!"
He has taught us the rules of Tibetan snooker:
The catch is you have to wait until next lifetime to play your shot.
This doesn't seem to bother Michael, who has worked his way
    to the photosynthesis section of the library.

These antics should not worry anyone,
Since we are all content here in the Shambhala shire.
We love our pink sandstone eighteenth-century spaceship,
Which has taken us on a great journey.
Even Matt, with his slagevar smile, is happy
As he makes us all a great big haggis and a bubble and squeak.

I toast you all—you're sweethearts,
Definitely the real Mukpo.

12 February 2004
The Tower of Lethendy, Scotland

HELP OTHERS

Why are some people happy, some sad?
Where does joy come from?
The secret is simple,
Always right in front of us.

That's the secret—
Help others, those in front of us.
If we help others,
We can do whatever we want.
All our lives we've been thinking backwards—
That to get what we want just takes thinking of "me."

A fool thinks about what "me" wants;
The wise think about what others want.
If we really want something, first we've got to give it away.
Satisfaction comes from helping others.
That's how to be a king, a queen.
That's what they say in Tibet.

16 February 2004
Heinsheim, Germany

STOP THE PAIN

I want to step out of self-infatuation,
Jump into big mind,
Leap into noble heart.
Noble means not wasting time,
Helping those in pain.

Stop doubting
Look at the world
See another's tears
Cry with him
Kiss her
Be who you are—one who cares.

Pain means too much attachment, holding on.
Attachment won't work out,
So let it go.
Help the whole world—let it go.
If you hesitate, remember—
You never had it anyway.

That's how to stop the pain—
Just like that.

17 February 2004
Heinsheim, Germany

WHAT ABOUT ME?

What about me?
That's my first thought every morning,
My last thought every night.
Has it gotten me anywhere—
More friends more love more joy?
By now I should be a bundle of joy,
Saying this mantra all day long.
It's like the beating of my heart:
What about me? What about me? What about me?

When I take a shower
I think, "What about me?
I hope this shower makes me feel happy."
When I bite into a donut
I say, "What about me?
I hope this donut makes me happy."

I hope this lover
This lunch
New suit
New tie
New jacket
Makes me happy.

I hope this new job
New house
New spiritual practice
New movie
New computer
New city
New country
New president

New planet
Makes me happy.

None of it will make me happy
Unless I do one simple thing:
Change "me" for "you":
Wake up in the morning, try something wild,
Break up the monotony and say,
"May you be happy,
You you you
May you be happy."

When I bite into this crisp apple
May you be happy.
When I give you a kiss
Drive my car
Make my bed—
May you be happy.
When I tie my shoelaces
Change the channel
Drink a latte with extra foam—
May it make you happy.
When I feel the sun and the breeze
Gaze into your eyes
Teach you the dharma—
May you be happy,

Know what?
When you're happy, I'm happy.
That's the formula—first you, then me.
Next time we say, "After you,"
It will mean something, because that's happiness—
A heart free of "What about me?"

18 February 2004
Heinsheim, Germany

AH HUM

Circle of time—
Everyone thinks they've gone somewhere.
Now it's midnight:
Between day and night love has finally begun.
It took time, but so does fate.

Hesitation never had a beginning
But tonight it had an end.
Time and space came to a point that we could feel, taste,
    and touch
Because of the movement of feet, hands, and heart.

This is something that has never happened before:
The Shambhala Heinsheim ceildh.
With a little bit of yogurt and yak fat thrown in,
It's a secret moment when we know we're in the best place
    possible.
Even though we're few and small,
This triumphant dance troop takes on the yak fat of the
    entire mandala.
They may not know it, but as we celebrate,
Millions of people are happy.

Why?
Because we celebrate dignity in life.
I'm happy to be here because everyone wants to be here—
We are the source of goodness.
Don't let it go to your head,
Just sing the warrior's cry, clear and loud.
This is your time—

Sing it clearly and precisely.
There has never been a better moment.

KI!
Subjugate all!
SO!
Make it inevitable!
LHA GYAL LO!
Let this moment be in your heart forever!
Happy and cheerful new year
From the indestructible castle of Heinsheim
To all sentient beings!

21 February 2004
Shambhala Day, Year of the Wood Monkey
Heinsheim, Germany

GIVE IT UP

Wealth, power, and fame—
Give it up.
We try so hard
To show that we're the one,
That we are really living
Only if we have wealth, power, and fame.

Wealth, power, and fame don't last.
They're here today, gone tomorrow.
Everyone who has it will lose it,
So why do we try in vain?
Get one—the other one goes,
Get all three—then get old.
Live in fear of losing it all
Chasing your tail,
Clinging to a rainbow.

Wealth, power, and fame—
Like summer clouds
Morning mist
First love
Evening rain
They come and go—
Give it up!

We think wealth will buy us freedom—
It keeps us bound to hope and fear.
We think power will bring control—
True power is controlling our mind.
Fame says we're okay,
But we're not quite sure we are.
Give it up!

If you want wealth,
Look into your heart for love and care.
It's like a jewel in a heap of dust—
Always there, rarely noticed.
This precious jewel will bring you wealth,
So discover who you are:
Unlock the richness in your heart.

If you want power, tame your mind.
Right now it rules—
Goes where it wants,
Thinks what it will.
Watch your mind and take control.
Own it
Rule it
Use it to generate wisdom and compassion—
That's real power.

If you want fame, help others.
Turn the world right side up—
Give up "all about me."
Kindness is king,
Compassion is queen.
Be famous for your love.

Now show the world you have enough:
Wealth of heart
Power of mind
Fame of kindness—
Don't give it up!

29 February 2004
Halifax, Nova Scotia

POETRY FINDS A DANCING PARTNER
(For Jamie Jewett and Thalia Field)

Protecting the earth,
The sky dancer is free.
Wild ponies of love
Gather in the highland meadow of coincidence.

This Mukpo's eyes open wide—
It's not often that poetry finds a dancing partner.
Even in Kalapa, the capital of Shambhala,
The windhorse of discursiveness has found a saddle.

Success requires wisdom.
Wisdom needs virtue.
When these friends kiss,
A child is born—friendship.

Who knows how to love?
As we know, love stands on the ground of space.
Take this freedom and play in it together.
Always remember—
It's about joy,
Delighting in the other.

This gentle being sends a kiss and a song—
May it bless you on this day!
Where the Tail of the Tiger
Envelops all with wildness and peace,
May this union show its rainbow.
Through these colors you will know
That everything is magic!

23 April 2004
Boulder, Colorado

SHIWA ÖKAR AND THE VALLEY OF WHITE

The white domain of Shiwa Ökar descended.
This gracious valley took the cosmic challenge
And blanketed with snow all fear and trepidation.
Now the youthful warrior surrounds
Our tiny palace of the Great Eastern Sun,
Humoring us as wind and snow six feet deep,
Halfway up the walls of my retreat.

Such abundant enthusiasm only demonstrates
How the dralas have anticipated us.
Holding back, they could wait no longer.
When we arrived, a polite kiss would have sufficed;
Instead they grabbed us with a drala bear hug.
Forgetting embarrassment we roll around on pure white ground,
Laughing so loud that our delight resounds as warrior cry:
KI and SO echo through the valley.

The world, preoccupied with selfish things,
Has no time to be snowbound—too much at stake.
Who is going to cut down the last tree
And suck the last drop of oil from the beautiful earth below our feet?
Inconceivable distance—basic goodness restrained—
Has been created by Shiwa Ökar's winter snowfall.

The Great Eastern Sun arose in this valley
And snow fell to welcome us.
No longer on Atlantic Standard Time,
We are not confused when snow welcomes sun,
For this is how warriors celebrate in Shambhala—
Snow with sun
Rock with tree

Men with women
Heaven with earth.
No ordinary consummation,
This snowfall is the beginning of a new kalpa.
The scorpion has manifested as a youthful boy and benevolent
    king,
A lover of space and time.
In this monumental blizzard,
The peaceful white light abhisheka descends:
Every snowflake gives transmission with a celestial white Ashe,
The kingdom of Shambhala contained within each crystal.
Let this snow melt in your mouth, truly quenching thirst.
Open your eyes—let it blind you with brilliance.
When this transmission is complete, only a rainbow will remain.
Looking closely you will see Shambhala vanishing into heaven.
That is where I go, for that is where I came from.

It is good to have a place to play
In the valley of Kalapa,
Where now I frolic in the pure white snow.
The message here is simple:
If I want to be free
I have no choice but to play in the pure domain of Shiwa Ökar.
For in reality there is one color only—white.
I am not in retreat—
I am discovering the universe in the werma smile of Shiwa Ökar,
My host for eternity.

25 January 2005
Kalapa Valley, Cape Breton

RETURN

Timing, the elixir of life,
Is not always predictable.
When snow fell thrice,
The turning point was uttered
In a giddy sigh,
A new beginning.

Now we have the release—
Constipation of conceptual concerns
Needed a new dawn.
The light has returned.

Upon this holy ground that many tribes fought over
Let us raise our arms in jolly salutation.
Let us puff our chests
Raise our plume
And stretch our wings.
Let us proclaim
Screech
And yell
Cock-a-doodle-doo!
KI KI!
SO SO!
Just proclaim this truth that we know to be right
In a foolish, rash, uncontained way.

Let us work together,
Gathering in hundreds and thousands.
What a spectacle this fellowship of warriors would make
If we flung embarrassment to the four winds

And decided
Life is all right and worth living.

9 February 2005
Shambhala Day, Year of the Wood Bird
Halifax, Nova Scotia

FREEDOM

Tantalizing, trepidatious,
Moving one foot in front of the other,
I am a runner—
There is no greater joy in the three worlds.
When lightning strikes the earth,
That is the cosmic step taking place.
When heart and lungs are placed in my hands,
Life depends on breathing and feeling.

Electricity comes forth in the sweat in my mouth—
Inspiration that allows me to traverse
Disbelief, laziness, daydreaming.
When I breathe,
All of those windfalls pass by as billowing clouds
Seen by a boat set sail across the waters
Of confusion, summer, and time.

Within this temporal journey details are important.
I taste the sweet smell of water with its eight qualities,
Respecting this gift for my human body.
I revel in having time and space to run among the gods.
No bounds—pure joy is my water bottle.
I am sustained with the ultimate elixir, my goo-ru.*
That vital inspiration sends me across this entire planet
With the pitter-patter of drala feet.

What bhumi can I not reach?
Placing my feet on the path, ripples affect the universe.
Therefore when I breathe,
I inhale all that is confused, degenerated, and unhappy.

When I exhale, my knee strikes high.
My Achilles is powerful, free from vulnerability.
Thus with the energy of surprise
I leap into this new dimension,
Seen only in the rapid movement of heart, feet, and mind.
May this moving experience be the source of all
  happiness.

*"Goo" is the high-carbohydrate gel that runners consume to sustain their energy.

14 March 2005
Singapore

THE OTHER SIDE OF A JASMINE CUP
(For Tseyang)

The sun broke through,
Camouflaged by speculation.
When the lips of realism
Smacked their kiss upon this bright being,
I was struck, overwhelmed, and mesmerized.
An infallible situation had gone awry.

When the cosmology of mercury reaches the boiling point
To which no sentimental waiter can offer lip service,
That is cupid's arrow donned by Genghis' feathers
Striking the center of mediacracy, the central valley,
While everyone in Hollywood tries to find a script to match.
Meanwhile I sit pleasantly upon my snow lion.

This may sound like a fantasy,
But it is as close to reality as we're going to get.
On the other side of a jasmine cup
Sits the delight of my unknown life.
I pay homage to her and what she may bring.
So lies destiny in the palm of her hand
As she sails between one stop and another
Through the grand stations of Paris.

That blue light of haphazard karmic fortuity
Might point to a mountaintop or the crest of my nose.
For now the destiny of companionship looms
Heavier than clouds in Hong Kong.
Having climbed to the mountaintop of capitalism,
Leaving only with the rosary of bodhi seeds in my hand,

I see that the world is full of surprises.
Now I know the biggest surprise:
There is truly a thing called love.

2 April 2005
Hong Kong

HOOK OF DELIGHT

The luminous rays of a moonlit kiss fell upon my life
When Yeshe, knower of everything good,
Swayed and moved across this busy monarch
Who was only hoping to catch a glimpse of the half-glowing moon.
Mesmerized by its full beauty, I could not sleep.
Perpetually drawn in by the hook of delight,
I knew it was you.

I am happy to give up on what I thought was freedom.
The world is a very small place;
You can only fly over it a few times.
Finally you catch your shadow,
See that nothing is changed.
When karma fell from the sky,
I thought it was an apple.

This evening warriors of the broken heart gather,
Having successfully climbed out of self-preservation's pool.
Knowing what's right and what to do,
Having good fortune and love,
We dance like mountain deer.

3 August 2005
Keystone, Colorado

Glossary

abhisheka (Sanskrit: sprinkle and pour) An empowerment in which a vajra master enters a student into the mandala of a particular deity.

AH HUM (Tibetan) Seed syllables representing the primordial essence of speech and mind.

anjali (Sanskrit) Placing hands together as in prayer.

Ashe (Tibetan: primordial stroke) The Shambhalian principle of innate human confidence; also the practice that invokes it in one stroke.

bhumi (Tibetan: *sa*; earth, stage, level) Usually refers to the ten stages on the path of a bodhisattva.

bodhichitta (Sanskrit: the heart/mind of enlightenment) The absolute principle of the essence of wakefulness existing in all beings: our basic nature of ultimate emptiness inseparable from compassion—radiant, unshakable, and impossible to formulate with concepts; also the relative aspiration, born of glimpsing our absolute nature, to practice the mahayana ("great vehicle" and deliver all sentient beings from samsara—the endless cycle of suffering—out of our compassion.

bodhisattva (Sanskrit: heart of awakened mind) One who has committed him- or herself to the mahayana path of compassion. One who relinquishes one's personal enlightenment to work for all sentient beings.

Chenrezig (Tibetan) The bodhisattva of compassion.

Chökyi Gyatso (Tibetan: ocean of dharma) The long form of Chögyam.
The Buddhist name of Sakyong Mipham Rinpoche's father, Vidyadhara
the Venerable Chögyam Trungpa Rinpoche.

dakini (Sanskrit: one who goes in the sky) A wrathful or semiwrathful
female deity, signifying compassion, emptiness, and wisdom. The dakinis
are tricky and playful, representing the basic space of fertility out of
which the play of relative existence arises.

dapön (Tibetan: arrow chief) A high ranking officer of the Dorje Kasung,
roughly equivalent to a Major in rank.

Dechen Chöling (Tibetan: dharma place of great bliss) A rural practice
and retreat center near Limoges, France.

Denma Gesar of Ling's chief warrior/minister. In wartime, he served as
Gesar's general; in peacetime, as minister.

dharmakaya (Sanskrit: the body of dharma) One of the three bodies of
buddhahood, this refers to enlightenment itself, wisdom beyond any
reference point—unoriginated, primordial mind, devoid of content.

dharmata (Tibetan: dharma-ness) The essence of reality, completely pure
nature.

Dombi Heruka One of the eighty-four great enlightened masters of the
Indian vajrayana ("indestructible vehicle") tradition.

Dorje Denma Ling (Tibetan: indestructible place of Denma) A rural practice and retreat center near Tatamagouche, Nova Scotia.

Dorje Dradül (Tibetan: indestructible warrior) The Shambhala name of
Chögyam Trungpa Rinpoche, Sakyong Mipham's father.

Dorje Kasung (Tibetan: indestructible command-protector.) The body of
practitioners in the Shambhala mandala who provide the container for
all Shambhala events, protecting the boundaries from disruption, and

who serve the principal teachers by safeguarding the decorum of their environment; also an individual member of that body. Kasung practice involves working with military forms to cultivate individual nonaggression, discipline, and sense of humor.

drala (Tibetan: above the enemy) The unconditioned wisdom and power of the world that exist simply in things as they are, beyond duality or aggression.

dütsi (Tibetan: deathless) Blessed liquor used in vajrayana meditation practices.

Eh ma! (Tibetan) An expression of wonder and joy.

garuda (Sanskrit) The king of birds, according to Tibetan legend, that hatches full-grown from its egg and soars into outer space, expanding and stretching its wings beyond any limits. This is the symbol of the third dignity of the Shambhala warrior, outrageousness, and represents the quality of freedom that arises from overcoming hope and fear.

Gesar of Ling The legendary warrior-king of Tibet, who lived in the eleventh century and ruled the provincial kingdom of Ling. The subject of the greatest epic of Tibetan literature, he is said to reside in Shambhala, from whence he will reappear, leading the armies of the twenty-fifth Rigden, to conquer the forces of darkness in a future age. Gesar is also said to belong to the Mukpo clan.

Great Eastern Sun Shambhalian symbol for the dawning of wisdom unobstructed by fear and negativity.

Kalapa The capital city of the mythical kingdom of Shambhala.

kalpa An extremely long time, sometimes calculated to be 4,320 million years.

Karmê-Chöling (Tibetan: dharma place of the Karma Kagyü) The rural practice and retreat center founded in Barnet, Vermont in 1970 by Chögyam Trungpa Rinpoche.

kasung See Dorje Kasung.

KI KI SO SO ASHE LHA GYALO (Tibetan: Ki Ki So So Ashe, may the divine ones be victorious) Shambhala warrior cry that rouses nonaggressive confidence.

lhasang (Tibetan: bringing down divine blessings ceremony) The juniper-smoke ceremony, which attracts the energy of drala.

Longchenpa A Tibetan meditation master (1308-64) who held the honor-ific "omniscient."

Magyal Pomra (Tibetan: gloriously collected king of horses) A local deity of eastern Tibet that was converted into a dharma protector by Padmasambhava. Magyal Pomra was one of the gate protectors of Surmang, Chögyam Trungpa's monastery in Tibet; he is also now the protector of Shambhala Mountain Center and Dorje Denma Ling.

mahamudra (Sanskrit: great seal, symbol, or gesture) The meditative transmis-sion handed down especially by the Kagyü school of Tibetan Buddhism. In this liberated state, all experiences are transformed into transcendent knowledge and skillful means. By resting our mind in the great luminosity of naturally arising primordial intelligence and energy, all of our ordinary experience becomes the vivid display of the enlightened mandala.

Milarepa The most famous yogi of Tibet (1025-1135).

Mukpo (Tibetan: dark brown) One of the six great tribes of eastern Tibet; Sakyong Mipham Rinpoche's family lineage.

OM VAJRASATTVA HUM (Sanskrit) A mantra recited to invoke Vajrasattva ("indestructible being"), a white buddha associated with purity.

OM VAJRA GURU PADMA SIDDI II HUM (Sanskrit) A mantra recited to invoke Padmasambhava ("the lotus-born"), the great teacher who brought the vajrayana teachings from India to Tibet in the eighth century.

prajna (Sanskrit: best knowledge) The intuitive wisdom that sees things as they are, cutting through conceptuality and dualism.

Rigden (Tibetan: possessor of the family) Embodiment of basic goodness, self-existing awareness. The name given to the twenty-five enlightened rulers of the legendary kingdom of Shambhala.

Sadhana of Mahamudra A text composed by Chögyam Trungpa Rinpoche before he arrived in the West, now practiced in Shambhala centers worldwide.

Sakyong (Tibetan: earth protector) The ruler who joins heaven and earth, vision and practicality, for the benefit of a good and sane human society; the Shambhala title first of Chögyam Trungpa Rinpoche, and now of Sakyong Mipham Rinpoche.

Samantabhadra (Sanskrit: all-good) The primordial, dharmakaya buddha, blue in color and naked, often depicted in union with a white wisdom consort.

shamatha (Sanskrit: peaceful abiding) The meditation practice of focusing the mind on the breath, cultivating awareness of thoughts as they come and go, and returning the mind to the breath.

Shambhala A legendary Himalayan kingdom, a place of peace and prosperity governed by wise and compassionate rulers. Also the name of the organization of which Sakyong Mipham Rinpoche is spiritual leader.

Shambhala Mountain Center A meditation center located in the Rocky Mountains, near Red Feather Lakes, Colorado.

Shiwa Ökar (Tibetan: peaceful white light) A youthful emanation of primordial confidence.

stupa (Sanskrit: hair knot) A characteristic expression of Buddhist architecture, often memorial monuments to the Buddha or other renowned teachers. The Sakyong's poems refer specifically to the Great Stupa of

Dharmakaya at Shambhala Mountain Center, built to honor his father and the introduction of Buddhism to the West.

TLGD Tiger Lion Garuda Dragon, symbols of the four dignities of the Shambhala warrior—Meek, Perky, Outrageous, and Inscrutable.

vajra (Sanskrit: indestructible) Symbol of true reality, emptiness, the adamantine being or essence of everything.

Vajrapani (Sanskrit: wielder of the vajra) The lord of mantra, also called Lord of Secret, Vajrapani is a bodhisattva depicted in both peaceful and wrathful forms.

vipashyana (Sanskrit: insight) The meditation practice of contemplating basic truths about existence, which leads to further realization.

warrior One who aspires to overcome self-obsession and negativity in order to uncover bodhichitta and act from for the benefit of others.

werma Gathering of enlightened drala.

windhorse The innate ability to attain success that occurs from acting virtuously.

Yeshe Tsogyal Princess of Kharchen, wisdom consort and chief disciple of Padmasambhava, who recorded his oral teachings.

About the Author

Born in India in 1962, Sakyong Mipham Rinpoche is the spiritual and family successor of his father, Vidyadhara the Venerable Chögyam Trungpa Rinpoche. He is the living holder of the Shambhala Buddhist tradition, a lineage that descends through his family, the Mukpo clan. This tradition emphasizes the basic goodness of all beings and teaches the art of courageous warriorship based on wisdom and compassion. The Sakyong is an incarnation of Mipham Jamyang Gyatso (1846–1912), one of the most revered meditation masters and scholars of Tibet. Educated in Buddhist meditation, philosophy, and ritual as well as calligraphy, poetry, and archery, Sakyong Mipham Rinpoche was raised in both Eastern and Western traditions. He holds the Nyingma and Kagyü lineages of Tibetan Buddhism. He teaches throughout the world.

For more information see Sakyong Mipham's Web site at www.mipham.com.